John Dewey's Essentials for Democracy and Education

Democracy and Education, by John Dewey, 1916

greatly abridged with contemporary comments and questions for application

By Dave Severson, Ed.D.

John Dewey's Essentials for
Democracy and Education

<u>Democracy and Education,</u>
by John Dewey, 1916
greatly abridged with contemporary comments
and questions for application

By Dave Severson, Ed.D.

Dedicated to my wife, Valeri, and to all the students over the years in the U.S. and in Europe who have taught me so much. Perhaps some of this book's content will contribute to whatever should have been taught to those students earlier, if only their teacher had been wiser.

Table of Contents

Biographical Notes: Psychologist, Philosopher, Educator

Dewey graduated from The University of Vermont in 1879, taught just three years of high school and it did not suit him. He earned a Ph.D. at Johns Hopkins in 1884.

He taught ten years at the University of Michigan, 1884-1894, and then taught ten years at the University of Chicago, 1894-1904. For the rest of his life he taught at Columbia University. He was as much a psychologist as a philosopher as an educator. His philosophical and political approach to issues is usually considered Pragmatic or Progressive. Socially he was active as a Humanist.

He was president of the American Psychological Association in 1899. He was president of the American Philosophical Association in 1905. He helped prevent a communist takeover of the American Federation of Teachers during his years of membership of that organization. He was also involved in forming a group which later became the NAACP.

Dewey was politically active, as well. He presided over the Dewey Hearings in Mexico in 1937 where a group of United States intellectuals attempted to exonerate Russian leader Leon Trotsky, convicted on charges from his previous trial in Moscow. Dewey died in 1952.

Progressive

Dewey's prominence was at the same time that Chicago was going through a prosperous time with architectural innovations in the huge buildings in commercial areas and there was burgeoning industry. Frank Lloyd Wright was among those designers. Upton Sinclair wrote The Jungle in 1906 exposing controversies in the meat packing industry.

During this progressive time with growth and development, which was somewhat tempered by the First World War, educators debated the purpose of education. As industry expanded and became more complex, there was a certain level of practical education needed for the work force. Other educational leaders argued that education should do more than just minimally prepare the workforce.

During the first quarter of the century, public education in rural areas was still very limited. Most people still considered an eighth grade education sufficient for farm and church needs. The author's mother had to insist on permission from her father to attend high school in 1922, rather than remain at home to help her mother raise the five younger siblings.

Since the numbers in higher education levels were not many, one might assume that a few pragmatic goals were all education was about. But you will find, as we study Dewey's positions, that he did not have a simplistic view of education. His opportunity was to influence the direction of education as it developed in this country and he addressed a complex array of issues.

So he looked beyond the national borders for inspiration. Dewey was greatly influence by the work of the German philosopher, Hegel. Hegelian philosophy was gaining in popularity.

Just prior to Hegel, philosophers had aligned themselves with either of two positions. One side held that conscious reason was all that needed to be discussed. The other side said that empirical realities are what life is about. Hegel tried to join the two into what he called Absolute Idealism. Hegel believed that as time and thought progress, people in society will progress in complexity of physical and spiritual development to where expanding government serves as a place for nurturing the advancing development for all. You will see this distinctly in the writings of Dewey.

Worth Studying

Why study the writings of John Dewey? In spite of his brief stint teaching pre-college, John Dewey exerted great influence on education thinking, and not without controversy. Perhaps because his intellect covered such a broad spectrum of psychology, philosophy and education, he could offer deeper suggestions for education, beyond just preparation for employment or classroom tips.

Why study his text? Everyone deserves to see primary source material and make their own interpretations. But why is this text so difficult to wade through? In the early 1900's educated people were expected to expound on their subject matter. Consider all those films of Teddy Roosevelt standing before people, thumbs in his vest, practicing his best elocution. Well, Dewey's book is full of it, elocution, that is.

Our new millennium

Times have changed. Some of the things Dewey protests are no longer threats to his positions. Technology is different. The knowledge base of education is different. Increased diversity in educational environments is different.

But human nature is the same. Social conflicts are the same. Differences of opinion on how much education is enough have not changed. Competition for resources is still an issue. As Dewey is paraphrased in this book, comments will be made relative to these changed or unchanged issues.

You may find that these ideas provoke change in your educational practice. It may cause you to question some attitudes that you encounter in your environment. Perhaps you, too, will develop additional perspectives to see beyond today's horizon, as you consider John Dewey's Essentials for Democracy and Education.

Rather than seeming like the study of Dewey is just a requirement in the curriculum, you may discover that it prompts authentic change and that it contributes to your own altruism as you perceive more deeply your significance as someone who acts deliberately on your environment.

Citations for source material are on the last page.

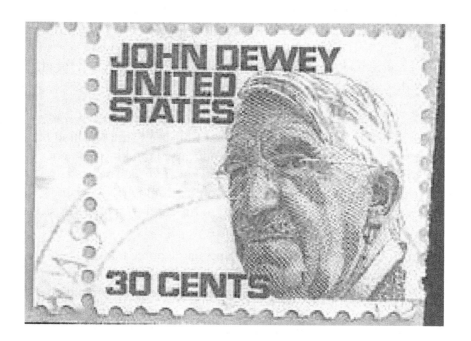

Introduction to the book,
<u>Democracy and Education.</u>

Dewey covers almost everything you could think of in dealing with the various facets of educational philosophy. His chapters thoughtfully conclude with a summary which is only slightly easier to understand than the chapter. Often, the summary, while more concise, is still vague.

Note: This book is a commentary. Great effort will be made to summarize, in modern language and in concise terms, what Dewey seems most interested in communicating. The balance of including plenty of direct quotation with the need to weed out extraneous material was a challenge. The reader is encouraged to refer to the original text for a more literal and more extensive investigation. The text is available for free online.

Note that some of his paragraphs are almost an entire page in length. He apparently was not trained to write a topic sentence with three supporting sentences. Although he always obeys the rule that a paragraph should always have at least three sentences, like this one does. Reading his words aloud with deliberate inflection may help you to keep the first part of a sentence in your short term memory until you eventually reach the period.

Some readers jump to the back of a book and read the ending first. His book does not have an ending. It seemingly just goes on and on until it runs out of pages. He has great ideas, but not succinct great ideas.

So let's just jump to the key to the book now. After reading the whole book, you may agree on the Big Idea. You will see some Hegel peeking through it. Feel free to choose another Big Idea if this one does not suit you.

THE BIG IDEA

The Big Idea for this book seems to be expressed in Chapter Seven: The Democratic Conception in Education. The eleventh paragraph begins with "Upon the educational side…" (Page numbers differ among book editions so, rather than use page number and footnotes, direct reference will be made by chapter and paragraph for all citations.)

"The devotion of democracy to education is a familiar fact. The superficial explanation is that a government resting upon popular suffrage cannot be successful unless those who elect and those who obey their governors are educated. Since a democratic society repudiates voluntary disposition and interest; these can only be created by education. But there is a deeper explanation. A democracy is more than a form of government; it is primarily a mode of associated living, of conjoint communicated experience. The extension in space of the number of individuals who participate in an instance so that each has to refer to his own action to that of others, and to consider the action of others to give point and direction to his own, is equivalent to the breaking down of those barriers class, race and national territory which kept men from perceiving the full import of their activity. These more numerous and more varied points of contact denote a greater diversity of stimuli to which an individual has to respond; they consequently put a premium on variation in his action. They secure a liberation of powers which remain suppressed as long as the incitations to action are partial, as they must be in a group which in its exclusiveness shuts out many interests."

In other words--Democracy is a social environment where everyone in their own individual way effects and is affected by everyone else. In a democracy, separations of class, race and ethnicity do not insulate you from the mutual involvement. In fact, the greater the variety of individuals, the greater will be the opportunity for you to see things more broadly and act on issues more comprehensively.

But the BIG IDEA has an extra booster.

In Chapter 4, paragraph 18, "3. The Educational Bearings of the Concept of Development."

"Our net conclusion is that life is development, and that developing, growing, is life. Translated into its educational equivalents, that means (i) that the educational process has no end beyond itself, it is its own end; and that (ii) the educational process is one of continual reorganizing, reconstructing, transforming."

In other words--Dewey believes that the main reason for education is to increase the capacity for the individual to learn more, in order to learn even more, and it requires radical absorption as the learner undergoes the continual, exponentially expanding and/or restructuring process of self development.

Conclusion:

When we combine the continuous development of the learner with the continuous mutual stimulation of a democratic social system, you have a Hegelian optimism that education is the free and dynamic force behind democratic social improvement, enriched by diversity.

That is a pretty big idea. In light of that, please consider the rest of Dewey's thoughts, chapter by chapter. And write out answers to the questions.

Chapter 1:
Education as a necessity of life

Living objects respond to adversity by adaptation. They use whatever resources are available. "Life is a self-renewing process through action upon the environment." Paragraph 2

A child has no preference for social standards. It is the job of the adults to inculcate those standards on the new generation. Dewey says that savages pass on skills and values through an apprenticeship. Such training is not adequate for developed societies, he says. Specialists have to be employed. Paragraph 6

"Men live in a community in virtue of the things which they have in common; and communication is the way they come to possess things in common." Paragraph 11 In today's world we acknowledge that a common understanding of terminology and paradigms is essential to a healthy organizational culture.

Yet as the industrial age burgeoned, Dewey saw the complexity as a challenge to experiential learning. He acknowledged that formal schooling had to play an essential role. "Much of what adults do is so remote in space and in meaning that playful imitation is less and less adequate to reproduce its spirit. Ability to share effectively in adult activities thus depends upon a prior training given with this end in view. Intentional agencies—schools—and explicit material—studied—are devised. The task of teaching certain things is delegated to a special group of persons." Paragraph 18

"Without such formal education it is not possible to transmit all the resources and achievements of a complex society. It also opens a way to a kind of experience which would not be accessible to the young, if they were left to pick up their training in informal association with others, since books and the symbols of knowledge are mastered." Paragraph 19

Ever wary of his educator colleagues, Dewey cautions, "Formal instruction, on the contrary, easily becomes remote and dead—abstract and bookish, to use the ordinary words of depreciation. What accumulated knowledge exists in low grade societies is at least put into practice; it is transmuted into character; it exists with the depth of meaning that attaches to its coming within urgent daily interests." Paragraph 20

The commonly held purpose of education, not endorsed by Dewey, is, "Thus we reach the ordinary notion of education: the notion which ignores its social necessity and its identity with all human association that affects conscious life, and which identifies it with imparting information about remote matters and the conveying of learning through verbal signs: the acquisition of literacy." Paragraph 21

However, Dewey argues for a balance between that type of factual schooling and a cultural transmission. "Hence one of the weightiest problems with which the philosophy of education has to cope is the method of keeping a proper balance between the informal and the formal, the incidental and the intentional, modes of education." Paragraph 22

His final comment, one often repeated, based on the growth in knowledge and technical skills of the recent few centuries, is a concern that education will become head knowledge, separated from experience in more direct situations. Paragraph 23

Questions for application:

1. Can you identify elements of the hard sciences (chemistry, physics) where cultural values have been integral parts of your lessons?

2. Has your math curriculum addressed cultural issues through statistics or graphing? What would that look like?

3. Can you cite instances where the curriculum did respond to cultural issues, but the lesson was designed to promote the interests of the dominant societal group? (For example: Is a gun safety course really just about gun safety or foundational for gun ownership issues?)

4. To what extent do you think the isolation of home schooling may be motivated by the inculcation of particular family bias or preferences?

Notes and Quotes:

Chapter 2.
Education as a Social Function

"In brief, the environment consists of those conditions that promote or hinder, stimulate or inhibit, the characteristic activities of a living being." Paragraph 4

"A being connected with other beings cannot perform his own activities without taking the activities of others into account. For they are the indispensable conditions of the realization of his tendencies. When he moves, he stirs them and reciprocally." Paragraph 5

"Now in many cases—too many cases—the activity of the immature human being is simply played upon to secure habits which are useful. He is trained like an animal rather than educated like a human being. His instincts remain attached to their original objects of pain or pleasure." Paragraph 7

Just existing in a society will cause some learning to happen but when adults try to impose a response pattern, the student develops unquestioning patterned reactions. Dewey wants to see the student engaged and accountable, not unlike the current expectations of accountable results. The difference in this century is that our schools are held accountable for test scores, causing educational direction to converge on test content. Dewey viewed education as a means for students to venture beyond an educational experience in divergent ways, as each pursues personal interests. He would look for accountability results to show how many different ways and how far students can develop their learning from one common curricular origin.

He sums up the desired student experience this way. "Setting up the conditions which stimulate certain visible and tangible ways of acting is the first step. Making the individual a sharer or partner in the associated activity so that he feels its success as his success, its failure as his failure, is the completing step." Paragraph 10

In spite of how verbose Dewey is, he then criticizes the lecture approach to learning, saying that language is not the delivery mechanism of learning.

"It would probably be admitted with little hesitation that a child gets the idea of, say, a hat by using it as other persons do; by covering the head with it, giving it to others to wear, having it put on by others when going out, etc." "After sounds have got meaning through connection with other things employed in a joint undertaking, they can be used in connection with other like sounds to develop new meanings, precisely as the things for which they stand are combined." Paragraph 11 and 14

That sounds like Dewey has been trained in the Total Physical Response (TPR) method of working with English Language Learners, but TPR was developed by Dr. Asher in San Jose in the 1970's.

There are elements in the context of general society which provide informal learning. First is language ability. Second is manners. Third is aesthetics. Here is a notable quote: "Example is notoriously more potent than precept. Good manners come, as we say, from good breeding or rather are good breeding; and breeding is acquired by habitual action, in response to habitual stimuli, not by conveying information." The third societal learning comes from being sensitive to aesthetics by being around art, music and finer things. For Dewey, squalid surroundings are as bad as over-decorated surroundings for developing appreciation of "harmonious objects". Paragraph 17

There are situations where school staff feel that the general society that students informally experience is not equipped to provide them with sufficient language tutelage, or appropriate behavior training or opportunity for appreciating good things. Some schools go so far as to promote "self-parenting" for children who must get themselves up, fed and off to school on time. Dewey would not disapprove of schools taking a dynamic role in these three areas. In fact, he insists that school experience should always include the component of social engagement. The crucial question remains, are these three areas taught at the school by precept or by example.

Why send children to school then? "In a precisely similar fashion, our daily associations cannot be trusted to make clear to the young the part played in our activities by remote physical energies, and by invisible structures. Hence a special mode of social intercourse is instituted, the school, to care for such matters." Paragraph 19

Remote physical energies in 1916 would likely include such things as electricity and radiation. Invisible structures may have included religion, government, or political consortiums.

Dewey calls on the schools to provide (1) a simplified environment, comprehensible to even the young. (2) Schools are to weed out elements of society that would limit the potential of the youth, a "purified medium of action." (3) The school is to provide a way for students to think about societal norms and question them, illuminated by the diversity provided by general society. Paragraphs 20, 21, 22

Questions for application

1. Dewey says schools should motivate engagement and they should hold students accountable. If the threat or promise of grades is used for motivation, in order to meet both of the above goals, is that sufficient to get student participation in your experience?

2. What assumptions do you make in getting to know your students regarding the evidence in their lives of effective learning in language ability, manners and aesthetic taste?

3. How does your school address "remote physical energies" and "invisible structures" in the way they are simplified, objectified to remove negative elements, and become matters of consideration and choice?

4. Would you agree that breeding is a process, rather than an event?

5. Do you see lesson plans that stimulate a student to action and engage that student to such an extent that due to ownership of the challenge the student demands his or her own persistence for success?

Notes and Quotes:

Chapter 3:
Education as Direction

In this chapter the three big terms are direction, control, and guidance. They form for Dewey "the general function of education".

Direction: "Focusing and ordering are thus the two aspects of direction, one spatial, the other temporal." It represents a consistent progress in a learning area. For someone with attention problems this would sound familiar: stick to the subject and get it done! Paragraph 4

Control: "Control, in truth, means only an empathic form of direction of powers, and covers the regulation gained by an individual through his own efforts quite as much as that brought about when others take the lead." It is about fostering a self-discipline in cooperation with the school.

Guidance: "The idea of assisting through cooperation the natural capacities of the individuals guided."

To sum up the beginning of the chapter, education, according to Dewey, should be student centered, coached to foster self-motivation and should facilitate the student to persist in a subject in a line of thought and action.

"Two conclusions emerge from these general statements. On the one hand, purely external direction is impossible. The environment can at most only supply stimuli to call out responses. These responses proceed from tendencies already possessed by the individual. Even when a person is frightened by threats into doing something, the threats work only because the person has an instinct of fear. If he has not, or if, though having it, it is under his own control, the threat has no more influence upon him than light has in causing a person to see who has no eyes. While the customs and rules of adults furnish stimuli which direct as well as evoke the activities of the young, the young, after all, participate in the direction which their actions finally take. In the strict sense, nothing can be forced upon them or into them." They either comply willingly or they comply out of fear, but adults cannot make them want to comply against their will. Paragraph 5

Dewey says that intellectual control "consists in the habits of understanding, that are set up in using objects in correspondence with others, whether by way of cooperation and assistance or rivalry and competition. Mind as a concrete thing is precisely the power to understand things in terms of the use made of them; a socialized mind is the power to understand them in terms of the use to which they are turned in joint or shared situations. And mind in this sense is the method of social control." Paragraph 21

In fewer words, Dewey seems to be saying that intellectual control comes in the understanding of the use of objects in ways that society finds acceptable, traditional. This may even go so far as to include "group think", where questioning does not happen. One of the dangers Dewey fears here is conformity by default. Dewey repects unity, not conformity.

Dewey draws some interesting thoughts about imitation. He says that it is unfortunate when people imitate the ends, but not the means. What students should imitate is the enquiry of an issue, not just the passing grade. If the passing grade is what is imitated, any process, authentic or not, will suffice. Students may rush through the job without time for reflection. They may copy from the work of others. If imitating the means is important, the student will benefit by the process of really learning the material, and possibly developing a divergent line of thought. Paragraph 31

A hundred years ago Dewey asked this about the unfortunate teaching practices of his contemporaries: "Why is it, in spite of the fact that teaching by pouring in, learning by a passive absorption, are universally condemned, that they are still so entrenched in practice?" For emphasis he adds, "That education is not an affair of 'telling' and being told, but an active and constructive process, is a principle almost as generally violated in practice as conceded in theory." Paragraph 34

Everybody knows better, but they lecture anyway!

"While books and conversation can do much, these agencies are usually relied upon too exclusively. Schools require for their full efficiency more opportunity for conjoint activities in which those instructed take part, so that they may acquire a social sense of their own powers and of the materials and appliances used." Paragraph 36

Dewey believes that true learning requires involvement and application. And as the applications take on greater social significance, their process is of greater learning value. That's why each of these chapters has questions for application. That's also why each chapter is followed by a notes and quotes page.

Questions for application

1. Direction, control, guidance: discuss how these elements are evident in your school environment.

2. What assumptions do you think exist in the school community which may constitute unquestioned group think?

3. When Dewey speaks of imitation of means, not of the ends, how would a teacher recognize that a student is learning, not just answering?

4. To what degree is lecturing disdained, yet practiced in your environment? Does your staff development person lecture teachers on the importance of active learning?

5. What practices can teachers use in the classroom to make sure that students are making application to a wider world? (For example: when a class collects canned food for a food drive, what portions of the campaign have been used to make subject matter more meaningful and, motivationally, to make the amount of food brought in to seem more vital and significant?)

Notes and Quotes:

Chapter 4:
Education as Growth

Dewey says that the nice thing about immaturity is that there is still a time for growth. A mature tree does not grow, and Dewey doesn't like things that can't grow a little more, all the time. He sees that a child's dependent status causes them to become interdependent with their surroundings, and you know by now that Dewey wants children to participate interdependently with the society around them.

He also sees a child as having plasticity, not yet set in his or her ways. There is still time to place the choices of interests and options of a diverse society before this developing citizen. The child is capable of developing dispositions and habits to pursue these choices.

Dewey has a higher regard for the word habits than we do. He is not referring to a habitual non-conscious act like fingernail chewing. "A habit is a form of executive skill, of efficiency of doing. A habit means an ability to use natural conditions as means to ends. It is an active control of the environment through control of the organs of action." Paragraph 11

In addition to the term habit representing a process skill, he insists that it make a difference, that it change something around it, that it take some control of the environment. Paragraph 12

Here is a fuller explanation by Dewey of habit: "It means formation of intellectual and emotional disposition as well as an increase in ease, economy and efficiency of action….it actively seeks for occasions to pass into full operation." Paragraph 15

Today we would probably substitute habit with the word practices or procedures, like when a physician practices medicine. It is a deliberate, skilled, cognitive way to affect one's surroundings; a fluency of skill.

In the same paragraph you will see his booster for the Big Idea of the book. "(i) that the educational process has no end beyond itself; it is its own end; and that (ii) the educational process is one of continual reorganizing, reconstructing, transforming." There was a second grade classroom with a sign over the classroom door stating, "This is a community of inquiry." That learning community just kept asking more questions and finding more answers.

Dewey says that routine habits, the definition of habits that we are familiar with, actually possess us, and hinder the plasticity that an active learner needs. Paragraph 16

Critical of people with the wrong attitude about immaturity and plasticity, Dewey describes them as thinking that: "Growth is regarded as having an end, rather than being an end." That group ignores, "instinctive or native powers of the young; …causes failure to develop initiative in coping with novel situations;….an undue emphasis on drill and other devices which secure automatic skill at the expense of personal perception." Paragraph 17

Remember, for Dewey the only goal of learning is to develop the capacity to learn more. His growth goal is to accomplish more growth.

He believes that if you regard immaturity as a lack of adult knowledge, you will educate students by pouring them full of knowledge until they have filled up to the adult level. That would be wrong. There is no adult "full" level if you believe in life-long learning. "Hence education means the enterprise of supplying the conditions which insure growth, or adequacy of life, irrespective of age." Paragraph 20

Questions for application

1. Address the issue of plasticity. To what extent is a child malleable, or is it an immutable fact that the acorn doesn't fall far from the tree?

2. To what extent do you make an effort to convince your students that they are engaged in the practice of literary inquiry rather than just reading, or that they are masterful manipulators in a digital context rather than doing arithmetic exercises? Do students see math as a descriptive language about how quantities change? How can you promote that more professional scholar attitude?

3. What are some of the routine, negating habits to try to eliminate in classrooms, such as students blurting out the answer before thinking time has elapsed? What classroom practices and procedures could students habituate to their advantage?

4. Are there things in your educational environment that encourage life-long learning, like Twilight School where adult education is visible by the children of those adults?

Notes and Quotes:

Chapter 5:

Preparation, Unfolding and Formal Discipline

While Dewey sees students as perpetually learning, he does not regard their status as candidates for adulthood, and the adult status as candidates for an afterlife. He sees the use of punishment as a negative during student days, that others tried to justify as being necessary in order to prepare students for adult life. He does not agree that punishment makes good adults. He sees the time used to try to coerce cooperation as a waste of good student years, a waste of valuable years of plasticity and interdependence. Paragraph 3

"If the environment, in school and out, supplies conditions which utilize adequately the present capacities of the immature, the future which grows out of the present is surely taken care of. The mistake is not in attaching importance to the preparation for future need, but in making it the mainspring of present effort. Because the need of preparation for a continually developing life is great, it is imperative that every energy should be bent to making the present experience as rich and significant as possible. Then as the present merges insensibly into the future, the future is taken care of." Dewey would not say, "Just learn it, because you will need it someday." His goal is that you would not teach for an unattached future, but instead teach for some present significance that is open ended enough to extend into the future to meet future needs. Paragraph 4

Unfolding is the process of asking leading questions of a student "to draw out" or to elicit a stream of inquiry where the student advances in learning and perhaps moves on in a direction of self-motivating interest. Dewey's caution is that it won't work without a student taking interest. Dewey concedes that with an unmotivated student, lecture might provide a few sticking points, at least, rather than leaving that student at the starting line. Paragraph 6

At this point in the chapter, Dewey goes into abundant detail on the philosophical applications of Hegel, Froebel, Locke and "the Greeks". If the philosophical approach is of interest, with discussions of "transcendental experiences" without an "a priori formula" that eventually moves on to where he discusses the fallacy of dualism, the "separation of activities and capacities from subject matter", then the reader should refer to original text.

"In concluding this portion of the discussion, note that the distinction between special and general education has nothing to do with the transferability of function or power. In the literal sense, any transfer is miraculous and impossible. But some activities are broad; they involve a coordination of many factors. Their development demands continuous alternation and readjustment. As conditions change, certain factors are subordinated, and others which had been of minor importance come to the front. There is constant redistribution of the focus of the action, as is seen in the illustration of a game as over against pulling a fixed weight by a series of uniform motions. Thus there is practice in prompt making of new combinations with the focus of activity shifted to meet change in subject matter." Paragraph 22

"The conception that the result of the educative process is capacity for further education stands in contrast with some of the ideas which have profoundly influenced educational practice." Paragraph 23

Over the hundred years since Dewey lectured on this, generations of jobs have been invented and become obsolete. How can you prepare for a future you cannot see? Dewey says you do it by making students into thoughtful, responsible, diligent, self-motivated, accountable consumers of perpetually reorganizing education. The enriched atmosphere of curiosity and adaptation, the open exchange of information, the recognition of need for change produce a responsiveness within a student that is essential to grow with the times.

Questions for application

1. In what ways could classroom or school discipline work against student enthusiasm for learning?

2. There are mental tasks and role-playing scenarios that can affect future learning, like teaching girls to play chess at elementary school so that they have good spatial reasoning ability when they take geometry. What other activities can take place in a classroom which would hold import later in another context?

3. How do you see that the purpose of education is to create "the capacity for further education" in the culture of your educational environment?

4. How do you balance mastery skills with the traits of adaptability that students will need in the future?

Notes and Quotes:

Chapter 6:
Education as Conservative and Progressive

Dewey appreciates the level of articulation of the educational philosophy of Herbart but ultimately regrets that this approach is like a schoolmaster who shows no regard for environmental sources of learning, something very significant to Dewey. Herbart would endorse the Great Books of History approach to enlightening the learner.

Because the Herbart position was so prevalent in higher education at the time, Dewey uses several pages to take exception to item after item. Dewey sees their view of the past as a reference of what not to do, not how to proceed. History builds on complexities that generate from each generation. Repeating history would be to go back in time, and Dewey's time, at the turn of the 20th century, had so much new technology that he felt new solutions were needed. The past was simply an advisor, not a pattern, to the present.

"The present, in short, generates the problems which lead us to search the past for suggestion and which supplies meaning to what we find when we search. The past is the past precisely because it does not include what is characteristic in the present. The moving present includes the past on condition that it uses the past to direct its own movement. The past is a great resource for imagination; it adds a new dimension to life, but on condition that it can be seen as the past of the present, not as another and disconnected world." Paragraph 13

"We thus reach a technical definition of education: It is that reconstruction or reorganization of experience which adds to the meaning of experience, and which increases the ability to direct the course of subsequent experience. (1) The increment of meaning corresponds to the increased perception of the connections and continuities of the activities in which we are engaged…. An activity which brings education or instruction with it makes one aware of some of the connections which had been imperceptible…. (2) The other side of an educative experience is an added power of subsequent direction or control. To say that one knows what he is about, or can intend certain consequences, is to say, of course, that he can better anticipate what is going to happen; that he can, therefore, get ready or prepare in advance so as to secure beneficial consequences and avert undesirable ones." Paragraph 15, 16

In other words, education technically increases our awareness of the context of our knowledge or thoughts, and increases our judgment of when and where to make proactive adjustments to our environment.

31

"A genuinely educative experience, then, one in which instruction is conveyed and ability increased, is contradistinguished from a routine activity on one hand, and a capricious activity on the other." In other words, the experience is not mindless repetition nor is it a silly thing. Paragraph 16

"The essential contrast of the idea of education as continuous reconstruction with the other one-sided conceptions which have been criticized in this and the previous chapter is that it identifies the end (the result) and the process. This is verbally self-contradictory, but only verbally. It means that experience as an active process occupies time and that its later period completes its earlier portion; it brings to light connections involved, but hitherto unperceived. The later outcome thus reveals the meaning of the earlier, while the experience as a whole establishes a bent or disposition toward the things possessing this meaning. Every such continuous activity is educative, and all education resides in having such experiences." Paragraph 17

To conclude, education should make a person increasingly aware of extensions of present knowledge, in response to present interests to the extent that a web of interrelatedness is recognized as the individual progresses in learning. That is progressive.

Questions for application:

1. To what extent do the lessons of the past induce our curricular intentions in the present?

2. There are universities that offer a Great Books major. If that were a teaching major, how would that approach to teaching differ from your own, and would Dewey like it?

3. Dewey speaks of education as a reconstruction of life experiences and how history points to the future. What potential area of redesign in your curriculum would invite reconstruction of current thought and projection about future development?

Notes and Quotes:

Chapter 7:
The Democratic Conception in Education

Perhaps the first six chapters of this book were introductory. This chapter seems to be what the book, Democracy and Education, would be about.

Every society that is functioning positively has "many interests consciously communicated and shared; and there are varied and free points of contact with other modes of association". Paragraph 4

In a despotic government fear is the primary motivator. "The real difficulty is that the appeal to fear is isolated." It inhibits the other elements essential to a healthy society. Paragraph 5

Dewey says that being subjected to despotic conditions is slavery. He quotes: "Plato defined a slave as one who accepts from another person the purposes which control his conduct... It is found wherever men are engaged in activity which is socially serviceable, but whose service they do not understand and have no personal interest in." Interest here means a personal stake. Paragraph 7

Remember, Dewey wrote at the time when union organizers were being murdered by coal mine operators. Workers in the steel mills were non-union. No one asked if they felt appreciated, and there were no focus groups to discuss ways to increase team effectiveness.

Cultural isolation was perceived by Dewey as a danger. "The essential point is that isolation makes for rigidity and formal institutionalizing of life, for static and selfish ideals within the (controlling) group." No wonder that union organizers were such a serious threat to the status quo. Paragraph 8

Paragraph 11 was already cited at the beginning of this book as essentially the Big Idea. A democracy is how people, with much in common, interact, honor differences, learn from listening, and find agreement. This is a powerful paragraph and should be read in its entirety.

"Upon the educational side we note first that the realization of a formal life in which interests are mutually interpenetrating, and where progress or readjustment, is an important consideration, makes a democratic community more interested than other communities have cause to be in deliberate and systematic education. The devotion of democracy to education is a familiar fact. The superficial explanation is that a government resting upon popular suffrage cannot be successful unless those who elect and who obey their governors are educated. Since a democratic society repudiates the principle of external authority, it must find a substitute in voluntary disposition and interest; these can be created only by education. But there is a deeper explanation. A democracy is more than a form of government; it is primarily a mode of associated living, of conjoint communicated experience. The extension in space of the number of individuals who participate in an interest so that each has to refer his own action to that of others, and to consider that action of others to give point and direction to his own, is equivalent to the breaking down of those barriers of class, race, and national territory which kept men from perceiving the full import of their activity. These more numerous and more varied points of contact denote a greater diversity of stimuli to which an individual has to respond; they consequently put a premium on variation in his action. They secure a liberation of powers which remain suppressed as long as the incitations to action are partial, as they must be in a group which in its exclusiveness shuts out many interests." Paragraph 11

Dewey also wants you to know about Plato. "No one could better express than did he the fact that a society is stably organized when each individual is doing that for which he has aptitude by nature in such a way as to be useful to others (or to contribute to the whole to which he belongs); and that it is the business of education to discover these aptitudes and progressively to train them for social use." Paragraph 13

Plato strongly influences Dewey's views about individual development. "We cannot better Plato's conviction that an individual is happy and society well organized when each individual engages in those activities for which he has a natural equipment, nor his conviction that it is the primary office of education to discover this equipment to its possessor and train him for its effective use." Paragraph 18

Dewey, however, is disappointed by the slave status tolerated in Greece. To him, a country espousing democracy but blind to slave vs. free status needed to struggle with the concept, if not to repudiate it entirely. The fact that they did not seem concerned causes Dewey to keep on searching.

Next comes Rousseau with the Rationalists in France and their goal of Cosmopolitanism. "Inquiry freed from prejudice and artificial restraints of church and state had revealed that the world is a scene of law…. Natural law would accomplish the same result in human relations, if men would only get rid of the artificial man-imposed coercive restrictions." But no institution would support such liberal thought. Paragraph 22

With the defeat of Napoleon, the German states perceived that they would only remain a dominant force if the population was well educated, and they established government funding for schooling. "The educational process was taken to be one of disciplinary training rather than of personal development." Personal development was subsumed into what was best for developing the State. This disappointed Dewey. Paragraph 25

Institutional sponsorship tends to favor education as a way to meet current needs. "Each generation is inclined to educate its young so as to get along in the present world instead of with a view to the proper end of education: the promotion of the best possible realization of humanity as humanity. Parents educate their children so that they may get on; princes educate their subjects as instruments of their own purposes." Paragraph 26

"Who, then, shall conduct education so that humanity may improve? We must depend upon the efforts of enlightened men in their private capacity. All culture begins with private men and spreads outward from them. Simply through the efforts of persons of enlarged inclinations, who are capable of grasping the ideal of a future better condition, is the gradual approximation of human nature to its end possible…. Rulers are simply interested in such training as will make their subjects better tools for their own intentions." Hence, benefactors, rather than sponsors, allow for freer expression of democratic developments. Paragraph 27

An educational system is dependent on the sociological geography where it takes place. "The concept of education as a social process and function has no definite meaning until we define the kind of society we have in mind." Paragraph 28

A second concluding point in this chapter is: "One of the fundamental problems in and for a democratic society is set by the conflict of a nationalistic and a wider social aim." Paragraph 29

 Education needs an institutional sponsor. If the sponsor is the nation or local government, there is a tendency for local immediate interests to dictate to the educational establishment. The extent of the democratic flexibility of the sponsor helps define the society that education represents.

Questions for application:

1. In Dewey's day, conformity to society was expected of immigrants. Today we are much more willing to allow ethnic differences to continue unchanged. Will the ethnic groups significantly changing American demographics these days "blend" in a democratic sense, honoring, learning, agreeing? How will that philosophical concept of inclusion become theirs in a pragmatic sense? How do we invite their participation in common democratic participation so that their sense of efficacy and empowerment discourages their participation in smaller groups conflicting for power (gangs)?

2. Dewey believes each child has different interests to develop. How do you allow for individualization in the classroom learning products? How do students identify their intellectual calling?

3. Regarding Dewey's disappointment with the German nationalized schooling goals, rather than schools helping to generate individual development, how does current high-stakes testing relate?

4. Some schools with religious sponsorship have clashed with local societies and politics in various countries. To what extent or in what way would you have consulted with them to help them achieve harmonious integration?

Notes and Quotes:

Chapter 8:
Aims in Education

It's time for a vocabulary lesson again. Dewey does not mean State Standards when he says aims. From now on, in studying Dewey's text, all educational aims are involved in the process of learning, not in completing some check-out from school.

An aim is not, "capricious or discontinuous action in the name of spontaneous self-expression. An aim implies an orderly and ordered activity, one in which the order consists in the progressive completing of a process.... A foresight of results." You should be able to say what you expect it will look like when the results are in. Paragraph 4

The function of knowing the end or having foresight influences the steps taken to reach an end. First, students look for assets and obstacles to reaching the end. Second, it informs the student of a probable sequence to arrive at the outcome. Third, knowing what the result should entail gives us direction in considering alternatives and in making a selection. Paragraph 5

"Acting with an aim is all one with acting intelligently.... To have a mind to do a thing is to foresee a future possibility; it is to have a plan for its accomplishment; it is to note the means which make the plan capable of execution and the obstructions in the way—or if it is really a *mind* to do the thing and not a vague aspiration—it is to have a plan which takes account of resources and difficulties. Mind is capacity to refer present conditions to future results, and future consequences to present conditions." Paragraph 7

To translate that a little, remember that back in Dewey's day, mind also meant a chosen intention or a determination. It does not here mean brain nor it does not mean obey. "I have a mind to set you on your head!" Do you have a mind to pass this class?

Dewey provides his criteria for good aims. Remember, that deep down inside, Dewey is a process man, not a product man. Remember that. A good aim has to have a context, a need, resources and obstacles. It has to have some idea of the end in sight. And it works its way through to an end. It is not solving the issue that counts for Dewey. It is the adventure of resolving the issue. Remember back a couple of chapters that Dewey said you should be an imitator of process, not a copier of the product?

"Education, as such, has no aims. Only persons, parents, and teachers, etc., have aims, not an abstract idea like education.... Even the most valid aims which can be put in words will, as words, do more harm than good unless one recognizes that they are not aims, but rather suggestions to educators as to how to observe, how to look ahead, and how to choose in liberating and directing the energies of the concrete situations in which they find themselves." Paragraph 14

This idea that aims should spring from within the student's personal interests reflects back on Dewey's statement that the goal should be to make perpetual learners, not skill managers for current technologies.

"In education, the currency of these externally imposed aims is responsible for the emphasis put upon the notion of preparation for a remote future and for rendering the work of both teacher and pupil mechanical and slavish." Paragraph 20

In other words, that fact that the teacher has to get the class to accomplish a list of State Standards with unimportant fact knowledge, using present day skills, and the urgency of the testing commencing after only 85% of the academic year is completed, yields a purpose for schools that may well be mechanical and slavish, not intrinsically purposeful and exponentially freeing. Dewey would say that is not good for kids.

Questions for application

1. Sometimes when students select a subject for an individual project for a science fair or a 4-H project, they have a situation which would allow for Dewey's concept of aim. What other learning situations have you seen where a true aim is prompted?

2. Dewey's second characteristic of a good aim is to have some "sketch" idea of what the outcome should be. How does that relate to developing a tolerance for ambiguity?

3. Describe learning situations you have participated in where the process was the goal, not the final product.

4. Which will have longer lasting benefit, process goals or product goals, and why?

5. Is there some part of the curriculum or school culture which is "mechanical and slavish" today? If so, can it be modified or eliminated?

Notes and Quotes:

Chapter 9:

Natural Development and Social Efficiency as Aims

"The wording of Rousseau will repay careful study. It contains as fundamental truths as have been uttered about education in conjunction with a curious twist. It would be impossible to say better what is said in the first sentences. The three factors of educative development are (a) the native structure of our bodily organs and their functional activities; (b) the uses to which the activities of these organs are put under the influence of other persons; (c) their direct interaction with the environment. This statement certainly covers the ground. His other two propositions are equally sound; namely, (a) that only when the three factors of education are consonant and cooperative does adequate development of the individual occur, and (b) that the native activities of the organs, being original, are basic in conceiving consonance." Paragraph 5

"In Rousseau's words: 'Children are always in motion; a sedentary life is injurious.' When he says that 'Nature's intention is to strengthen the body before exercising the mind' he hardly states the fact fairly. But if he had said that nature's 'intention' (to adopt his poetical form of speech) is to develop the mind especially by exercise of the muscles of the body he would have stated a positive fact. In other words, the aim of following nature means, in the concrete, regard for the actual part played by use of the bodily organs in explorations, in handling of materials, in plays and games." Paragraph 9

"It is a fact that we must look to the activities and achievements of associated life to find what the development of power—that is to say, efficiency—means. The error is in implying that we must adopt measures of subordination rather than of utilization to secure efficiency. The doctrine is rendered adequate when we recognize that social efficiency is attained not by negative constraint but by positive use of native individual capacities in occupations having a social meaning." In other words, active listening, patience and reflection, stating points to ponder, are expressions of social efficiency in daily dialogue. Paragraph 15

"It must be borne in mind that ultimately social efficiency means neither more nor less than capacity to share in a give and take of experience. It covers all that makes one's own experience more worthwhile to others, and all that enables one to participate more richly in the worthwhile experiences of others. Ability to produce and to enjoy art, capacity for recreation, the significant utilization of leisure, are more important elements in it than elements conventionally associated oftentimes with citizenship." Paragraph 19

"In the broadest sense, social efficiency is nothing less than that socialization of mind which is actively concerned in making experiences more communicable; in breaking down the barriers of social stratification which make individuals impervious to the interests of others." Paragraph 20

"The aim of efficiency (like any educational aim) must be included within the process of experience. When it is measured by tangible external products, and not by the achieving of a distinctively valuable experience, it becomes materialistic. Results in the way of commodities which may be the outgrowth of an efficient personality are, in the strictest sense, by-products of education; by-products which are inevitable and important, but nevertheless by-products. To set up an external aim strengthens by reaction the false conception of culture which identifies it with something purely 'inner'. And the idea of perfecting an 'inner' personality is a sure sign of social divisions. What is called inner is simply that which does not connect with others—which is not capable of free and full communication." You don't get to be alone on a desert island. You bump into people all the time and they affect you and you affect them, so there's little that is "inner" about you. Paragraph 23

"It is the particular task of education at the present time to struggle in behalf of an aim in which social efficiency and personal culture are synonyms instead of antagonists." Paragraph 24

"But social efficiency as an educational purpose should mean cultivation of power to join freely and fully in shared or common activities. This is impossible without culture, while it brings a reward in culture, because one cannot share in intercourse with others without learning—without getting a broader point of view and perceiving things of which one would otherwise be ignorant. And there is perhaps no better definition of culture than that it is the capacity for constantly expanding the range and accuracy of one's perception of meanings." Paragraph 25

Questions for application

1. Dewey starts out saying that efficiency means 'development of power'. How would you describe his positive approach to a power that would affect the world around you?

2. How would Dewey describe cooperative group activities with regard to his definition of social efficiency?

3. How would you describe a parallel sense to 'social efficiency' and the phrase 'travel is broadening'?

Notes and Quotes:

Chapter 10:
Interest and Discipline

Interest

Dewey starts the chapter contrasting the level of investment of personal concern using the example of a person in prison watching passively as the rain comes down outside his cell, compared to the level of concern of a father planning an outing with the family which the rain threatens to cancel.

"Interest and aims, concern and purpose, are necessarily connected. Such words as aim, intent, end, emphasize the results which are wanted and striven for; they take for granted the personal attitude of solicitude and attentive eagerness. Such words as interest, affection, concern, motivation, emphasize the bearing of what is foreseen upon the individual's fortunes, and his active desire to act to secure a possible result.... We may call the phase of personal concern emotional and volitional, but there is no separation in the facts of the situation." Paragraph 2

Dewey would not disagree that personal motivation often is based on "What's in it for me?" When Dewey addresses the development on individual interest in learning, he notes that many educators rely on some shallow seductiveness, like a bribe, to generate interests of the learners. This he calls "soft" pedagogy, or "soup kitchen" pedagogy. Today we would often refer to this as external motivation. Paragraph 5

Discipline

"It is obvious that a very large part of the everyday meaning of will is precisely the deliberate or conscious disposition to persist and endure in a planned course of actions in spite of difficulties and contrary solicitations." Paragraph 9

"A person who is trained to consider his actions, to undertake them deliberately, is in so far forth disciplined. Add to this ability a power to endure in an intelligently chosen course in face of distraction, confusion, and difficulty, and you have the essence of discipline." Paragraph 12

We would probably say that discipline for Dewey is focused persistence. It represents the intention and the will to pursue a task until completion. He regards it as a positive trait.

"Interest" is the motivation, "discipline" is the pursuit, of the "aim". "Interest represents the moving force of objects... in any experience having a purpose." Without interest, "Subject matter is then regarded as something complete in itself; it is just something to be learned or known..." Paragraph 14

Then Dewey goes back to a discussion of his meaning of "mind" as a purpose or intention. He reviews it with this definition, "it is a name for a course of action in so far as that is intelligently directed; in so far, that is to say, as aims, ends, enter into it, with selection of means to further the attainment of aims." He continues to say that people do not possess a static quality of intelligence, but their actions may be intelligently done. Paragraph 18

But how do you inculcate interest and discipline? "The problem of instruction is thus that of finding material which will engage a person in specific activities having an aim or purpose of moment or interest to him, and dealing with things not as gymnastic appliances but as conditions for the attainment of ends." Dewey further cautions against thinking that isolating some sub-discipline will be any more effective in engaging the learner. Paragraph 19

Good curriculum is not about the teacher's today; it is about the learner's tomorrow. The learner is the primary stakeholder, and there is no perceived value for a stakeholder if there is no perceived relevance to a pending pay-off from persisting in learning.

Dewey cites historical curriculum as being erroneous in two ways. The first way is by establishing a course of study that remains unquestioned and unchanged. Under that system, students who fail, do so because they are at fault. "The responsibility was transferred from the educator to the pupil because the material did not have to meet specific tests; it did not have to be shown that it fulfilled any particular need or served any specific end. It was designed to be discipline in general, and if it failed, it was because the individual was unwilling to be disciplined." Some people have felt that was the case in the assignment to study the writings of John Dewey! Paragraph 20

The other unfortunate error in curriculum is studying subject matter as distinctly separate courses, without regard for the fact that life requires an effective person to integrate the various skills and abilities to meet real world situations. This is consistent with Dewey's discussion of aims, the pursuit of interests without boundaries of subject matter differences. Paragraph 22

Dewey was very involved with social issues and causes of the time, applications of his aims. It is not surprising that he draws the reader into a level of social consciousness during the study of this book. He warns that intellectual pursuits

49

can be an escape from the world, benefiting no one else. "…their feelings and ideas are turned upon themselves, instead of being methods in acts which modify conditions. Their mental life is sentimental; an enjoyment of an inner landscape. Even the pursuit of science may become an asylum of refuge from the hard conditions of life—not a temporary retreat for the sake of recuperation and clarification in true dealings with the world." Paragraph 24

Sometimes the academic community is accused of exactly this issue. Dewey seems to say that brain candy is permitted for a temporary retreat but only for preparation to return to the real world. For him, liberal arts study and real world application is essential.

Drawing the reader further into the social issues, Dewey describes the state of schooling in the early 20th century. How different from our experience does it sound, nearly 100 years later? "It throws light upon the clash of aims manifested in different portions of the school system; the narrowly disciplinary or cultural character of most elementary education, the narrowly disciplinary or cultural character of most higher education." Paragraph 26

"But it also helps define the peculiar problem of present education. The school cannot immediately escape from the ideals set by prior social conditions. But it should contribute through the type of intellectual and emotion disposition which it forms to the improvement of those conditions. And just here the true conceptions of interest and discipline are full of significance. Persons whose interests have been enlarged and intelligence trained by dealing with things and facts in active occupations having a purpose (whether in play or in work) will be those more likely to escape the alternatives of an academic and aloof knowledge and a hard, narrow, and merely 'practical' practice." Paragraph 27

While many regarded Dewey as controversial or radical in his progressive views, he states that he is actually in the middle ground, between aloof academia and pedantic apprenticeship.

Questions for application

1. Two teachers attempt to establish "interest" in preparation for studying animals that their students will see at the zoo field trip. One teacher brings a paper bag and has a small stuffed animal in it. Students enjoy trying to guess what's in the bag. Another teacher shows a promotional video of the zoo and asks students to pick an animal to study before the trip with the role assignment that they will act as class docents for those animals when the class visits the zoo. Identify the level of engagement in the "interest" elements in these two approaches.

2. In Dewey's discussion of discipline, he mentions distraction, confusion and difficulty. Comment on the issue of shortened attention spans, frustration with studies and length of assignments: how would you allow students to develop perseverance without letting the task of learning inflict those obstacles on students?

3. In the curriculum you work with, to what extent is the learning task a matter of established pattern rather than a response to a recognized contemporary need and interest?

Notes and Quotes:

Chapter 11:
Experience and Thinking

"The nature of experience can be understood only by noting that it includes an active and a passive element peculiarly combined. On the active hand, experience is trying—a meaning which is made explicit in the connected term experiment. On the passive, it is undergoing. When we experience something we act upon it, we do something with it; then we suffer or undergo the consequences. We do something to the thing and then it does something to us in return: such is the peculiar combination. The connection of these two phases of experience measures the fruitfulness of value of the experience.... When the change made by action is reflected back into a change made in us, the mere flux is loaded with significance." Learning happens when action provides feedback. Paragraph 1

When we do things without deliberation, they are activities without learning. When things happen to us which we did not design and which we do not reflect on, they are accidents, not causes of learning. Only two directional meaning, the cause and it's affect on us, are sources of learning. Imparting facts does not produce significant learning. In this situation, the question "So what?" may be the best test of deliberate stimulus and reflection on response. Paragraph 2

You may recall that Dewey only taught high school for four years before moving on to university teaching. Perhaps those few high school years were not so good in Dewey's experience. Consider his account of how things go when students and schooling are not well matched.

"The nervous strain and fatigue which result with both teacher and pupil are a necessary consequence of the abnormality of the situation in which bodily activity is divorced from the perception of meaning. Callous indifference and explosions from strain alternate. The neglected body, having no organized fruitful channels of activity, breaks forth, without knowing why or how, into meaningless boisterousness, or settles into equally meaningless fooling—both very different from the normal play of children. Physically active children become active and unruly; the more quiescent, so-called conscientious ones spend what energy they have in the negative task of keeping their instincts and active tendencies suppressed, instead of in a positive one of constructive planning and execution; they are thus educated not into responsibility for the significant and graceful use of bodily powers, but into an enforced duty not to give them free play." Paragraph 5

Dewey sees effective educational experience as creating a web of interconnected meanings. He sees experiences leading to practices, developing and testing theories and resulting in established facts, which lead the learner on to new complexities and learning endeavors. Interrelationships make learning significant and broadly applicable to real life applications.

"Words, the counters for ideas, are, however, easily taken for ideas..... But we are very easily trained to be content with a minimum of meaning, and fail to take note of how restricted is our perception of the relations which confer significance. We get so thoroughly used to a kind of pseudo-idea, a half perception, that we are not aware how half-dead our mental action is and how much keener and more extensive our observations and ideas would be if we formed them under conditions of a vital experience which required us to use judgment: to hunt for the connections of the thing dealt with." Paragraph 9

Dewey is obviously strongly opposed to didactic teaching. "An ounce of experience is better than a ton of theory simply because it is only in experience that any theory has vital and verifiable significance. An experience, a very humble experience, is capable of generating and carrying any amount of theory (or intellectual comment), but a theory apart from an experience cannot be definitely grasped even as theory." Paragraph 10

While Dewey is tolerant of trial and error experience because it may generate some learning, he would rather have estimation, combining reasoning and anticipation, than guestimation, which is a stab in the dark. "We analyze to see just what lies between so as to bind together cause and effect, activity and consequence. This extension of our insight makes foresight more accurate and comprehensive." In other words, use your insight to build your foresight. Paragraph 11

Dewey offers this definition of thinking. "Thinking, in other words, is the intentional endeavor to discover specific connections between something which we do and the consequences which result, so that the two become continuous." Paragraph 12

"The opposites, once more, to thoughtful action are routine and capricious behavior." Both routine and capricious behaviors "refuse to acknowledge responsibility for the future consequences which flow from present action. Reflection is the acceptance of such responsibility." Word searches and cartoon videos generally do not lead students to higher or deeper thought. Paragraph 13

Dewey says that reflection and risk are part of thinking. The reflection is about what eventual affect will result, the risk is that the result will not be a desirable result. But when a situation is incomplete, there is a need to proceed. "All thinking is research, and all research is native, original, with him who carries it on, even if everybody else in the world already is sure of what he is still looking for." Paragraph 16

The effect of the reflection on the situation, the risk of thinking correctly or not, the research incumbent on preparing a conclusion regarding an unclear situation leaves a student in an acceptable state of doubt. "Systematic advance in invention and discovery began when men recognized that they could utilize doubt for purposes of inquiry by forming conjectures to guide action in tentative explorations, whose development would confirm, refute, or modify the guiding conjecture. While the Greeks made knowledge more than learning, modern science makes conserved knowledge only a means to learning, to discovery" Paragraph 17

Eventually Dewey arrives at a sequence to the fruits of reflection. First comes doubt, then an anticipated result, then research, then refinement and finally taking a stand. Paragraph 20

Questions for application:

1. How do you think Dewey would contrast the two terms: definition and meaning?

2. In a sixth grade classroom students were asked to suggest how many marbles were in a large glass jar. With each suggestion, which ranged from 20 to 3000, the teachers said, "That's a possibility." How would Dewey have encouraged inquiry, feedback, reasoning and reflection?

3. In your learning community, itemize three situations this week where the five fruits of reflection were evident. (This is the last item on the previous page. The fruits seem a lot like the scientific method.)

4. Where do you observe resistance to learning where risk taking may be an issue? Where do you observe resistance to teaching where risk taking may be an issue? Where do you observe resistance to administrative leadership where risk taking may be an issue?

5. If you agree that learning comes from experience, how do you learn about things you read about? Describe the necessary conditions of dynamic vicarious experiences (for example: emotional content, urgency of purpose, or drama of presentation). Do your study materials meet those conditions?

Notes and Quotes:

Chapter 12:
Thinking in Education

"The parceling out of instruction among various ends such as acquisition of skill (in reading, spelling, writing, drawing, reciting); acquiring information (in history and geography), and training of thinking is a measure of the ineffective way in which we accomplish all three. Thinking which is not connected with increase of efficiency in action, and with learning more about ourselves and the world in which we live, has something the matter with it just as thought. And skill obtained apart from thinking is not connected with any sense of the purposes for which it is to be used." This is a reference to his comments about routine or capricious efforts he would designate as non-learning. Paragraph 1

"The sole direct path to enduring improvement in the methods of instruction and learning consists in centering upon the conditions which exact, promote, and test thinking. Thinking is the method of intelligent learning, of learning that employs and rewards mind. We speak, legitimately enough, about the method of thinking, but the important thing to bear in mind about method is that thinking is method, the method of intelligent experience in the course which it takes." Paragraph 1

That may sound like doubletalk: method of thinking and thinking is method. Basically he is referring to following a thread of intelligent experience. Previous exposure to the academic topic is not experience. It may be reference, but even the prior knowledge may not have been the type of informative experience that Dewey is looking for. He warns that educators too often incorrectly assume an experience base in their students. Paragraph 3

Successful learning methods in all subject areas "depend for their efficiency upon the fact that they go back to the type of the situation which causes reflection out of school in ordinary life. They give the pupils something to do, not something to learn; and the doing is of such a nature as to demand thinking, or the intentional noting of connections; learning naturally results." Paragraph 4

Regarding connection with the real world, Dewey has this to say. "No one has ever explained why children are so full of questions outside of the school (so that they pester grown-up persons if they get any encouragement), and the conspicuous absence of display of curiosity about the subject matter of school lessons." Paragraph 7

If you ask a group of adults to reflect back on their most profound learning experience, most of them will cite a situation in a non-school setting. For one, it may have been learning leadership skills in the Scouts. For another it may have been the discipline of a long term 4-H project. For another it may have been the humiliating consequences after a shop-lifting experience. A profound learning memory was probably not a graphing assignment in algebra.

"The material of thinking is not thoughts, but actions, facts, events, and the relations of things." How large a learning challenge is too large? Teachers need to structure a challenge. "A large part of the art of instruction lies in making the difficulty of new problems large enough to challenge thought, and small enough so that, in addition to the confusion naturally attending the novel elements, there shall be luminous familiar spots from which helpful suggestions may spring." Students need sufficient data (materials of thought) and they need to work in their proximal zone of development (large enough and small enough). That sounds pretty contemporary. Paragraph 9

"A well trained mind is one that has a maximum of resources behind it, so to speak, and that is accustomed to go over its past experiences to see what they yield." Paragraph 10

"There is no inconsistency in saying that in schools there is usually both too much and too little information supplied by others. The accumulation and acquisition of information for purposes of reproduction in recitation and examination is made too much of…. No one could construct a house on ground cluttered with miscellaneous junk. Pupils who have stored their 'minds' with all kinds of material which they have never put to intellectual uses are sure to be hampered when they try to think." Paragraph 11

"The correlate in thinking of facts, data, knowledge already acquired, is suggestions, inferences, conjectured meanings, suppositions, tentative explanations:--ideas, in short… They forecast possible results, things to do, not facts (things already done). Inference is always an invasion of the unknown, a leap from the known." Paragraph 12

"When Newton thought of his theory of gravitation, the creative aspect of his thought was not found in its materials. They were familiar; many of them commonplace—sun, moon, planets, weight, distance, mass, square of numbers. These were not original ideas; they were established facts. His originality lay in the use to which these familiar acquaintances were put by introduction into an unfamiliar context. The same is true of every striking scientific discovery, every great invention, every admirable artistic production. Only silly folk identify creative originality with the extraordinary and fanciful; others recognize that its

59

measure lies in putting everyday things to uses which had not occurred to others. The operation is novel, not the materials out of which it is constructed." Paragraph 13

For Dewey, learning is always active and applied. "This does not mean that the teacher is to stand off and look on; the alternative to furnishing ready-made subject matter and listening to the accuracy with which it is reproduced is not quiescence, but participation, sharing, in an activity. In such shared activity, the teacher s a learner, and the learner is, without knowing it, a teacher—and upon the whole, the less consciousness there is, on either side, of either giving or receiving instruction, the better." Paragraph 15

Dewey disdains people's high regard for thoughts. He says that you cannot test a thought, but you can test an idea. So for him, having the idea is more useful than having a thought. However, he does not see idea generating, rather than unprocessed thought, as a universal expectation in the educational considerations of his day. This reflects back again at the fact that Dewey is a process man, not a product man. Paragraph 17

"While it is desirable that all educational institutions should be equipped so as to give students an opportunity for acquiring and testing ideas and information in active pursuits typifying important social situations, it will, doubtless, be a long time before all of them are thus furnished…. Classroom instruction falls into three kinds. The least desirable treats each lesson as an independent whole. It does not put upon the student the responsibility of finding points of contact between it and other lessons in the same subject, or other subjects of study. Wiser teachers see to it that the student is systematically led to utilize his earlier lessons to help understand the present one, and also to use the present to throw additional light upon what has already been acquired. Results are better, but school subject matter is still isolated. Save by accident, out-of-school experience is left in its crude and comparatively irreflective state. It is not subject to the refining and expanding influences of the more accurate and comprehensive material of direct instruction. The latter is not motivated and impregnated with a sense of reality by being intermingled with the realities of everyday life. The best type of teaching bears in mind the desirability of affecting this interconnection. It puts the student in the habitual attitude of finding points of contact and mutual bearings." Paragraph 21

Questions for application

1. Many teachers open a lesson by referring the students to prior knowledge. Often they refer to a previous lesson where only half of the class attained mastery, yet all are expected to link the new lesson onto a lesson that half of them don't possess. This makes Dewey frown. Rather, what five prior universal experiences could you have referred to in the learning situations where you spend your time?

2. What sort of stimulation is needed to get students to ask "pestering questions"?

3. Where did your most profound learning experience take place? How could your student bring their out-of-school experiences into the classroom for further learning?

4. How have you been able to teach a concept so broadly that you were able to have the student approach it from several perspectives and interests? (For example, using the author's book, Figure It Out Faster with the Twelve Bridges to Meaning.)

Notes and Quotes:

The best type of teaching
connects a sense of reality
w/ the realities of everyday
life. (p.60)

YouTube: wing Tech... teachers using tech to connect learning
to real life environmental issues

YouTube: teaching methods for inspiring...
-choice -collaboration -communication -critical thinking
    & creativity   (problem solving)
    ⌐→we're wired for free will   we're social creatures

NEA: all but choice are essential 21st cent. skills

Chapter 13:
The Nature of Method

"The trinity of school topics is <u>subject matter</u>, <u>methods</u>, and <u>administration</u> or government. We have been concerned with the two former in recent chapters. It remains to disentangle them from the context in which they have been referred to, and discuss explicitly their nature." Paragraph 1

"The statement that method means directed movement of subject matter towards ends is formal." Paragraph 4

"Experience as the perception of the connection between something tried and something undergone in consequence is a process. Apart from effort to control the course which the process takes, there is no distinction of subject matter and method. There is simply an activity which includes both what an individual does and what the environment does." Paragraph 5

For Dewey, subject matter and method are so closely linked, it is like a noun form and a verb form. "There is the thing seen, heard, loved, hated, imagined, and there is the act of seeing, hearing, loving, hating, imagining…." the thing. Paragraph 6

Individualized motivation and pursuit of interests are of intense concern for Dewey. But he saw that education can provide some of the lifespan of other people's experiences as general methods available to all. "Part of his learning, a very important part, consists in becoming master of the methods which the experience of others has shown to be more efficient in like cases of getting knowledge. The general methods are in no way opposed to individual initiative and originality—to personal ways of doing things. On the contrary they are reinforcements of them. For there is a radical difference between even the most general method and a prescribed rule. The latter is a direct guide to action; the former operates indirectly through the enlightenment it supplies as to ends and means." Paragraph 15

He warns that learning from the experiences of experts can be an efficient way to grasp how things worked out for them. The learner must remember that it was the expert's experience. It is the application of that experience to the learner's world that determines if it is "of worth or of harm according as they make his personal reaction more intelligent or as they induce a person to dispense with exercise of his own judgment." Let their experience advise you, not their opinion. Paragraph 17

This is a faint reference to what Dewey said about history, several chapters back. We do not learn history because it is a pattern to repeat. We use it as reference to make our own new combination of concepts to deal with the present situation. Dewey will use experts but retains the right to extend his thoughts beyond their experiences.

Dewey regards all students as learners, without differing status. He feels strongly about it. The whole paragraph will have to be quoted because this is a major statement. No student is relegated to "average", and no student is filled with pride, or advanced classification, because of a high score on a contrived test based on an accepted "method" of the tester's choosing.

"If what was said earlier about originality of thought seemed overstrained, demanding more of education than the capacities of average human nature permit, the difficulty is that we lie under the incubus of a superstition. We have set up the notion of mind at large, of intellectual method that is the same for all. Then we regard individuals as differing in the quantity of mind with which they are charged. Ordinary persons are then expected to be ordinary. Only the exceptional are allowed to have originality. The measure of difference between the average student and the genius is a measure of the absence of originality in the former. But this notion of mind in general is a fiction. How one person's abilities compare in quantity with those of another is none of the teacher's business. It is irrelevant to his work. What is required is that every individual shall have opportunities to employ his own powers in activities that have meaning. Mind, individual method, originality (these are convertible terms) signify the quality of purposive or directed action. If we act upon this conviction, we shall secure more originality even by the conventional standard than now develops. Imposing an alleged uniform general method upon everybody breeds mediocrity in all but the very exceptional. And measuring originality by deviation from the mass breeds eccentricity in them. Thus we stifle the distinctive quality of the many, and save in rare instances (like, say, that of Darwin) infect the rare geniuses with an unwholesome quality."
Paragraph 18

So, differentiate the curriculum. Allow for individual interests, individual methods of intellectual pursuit. Because of the individualized base, originality will happen more than if students perform a pattern prescribed by a teacher. And don't let the GATE students think they are of a different social or intellectual class. This book is about democracy. Dewey doesn't want to fall into Plato's assumption of a class system.

The most general features of the method of the reflective situation are "problem, collection and analysis of data, projection and elaboration of suggestions or ideas, experimental application and testing; the resulting conclusion or judgment." Personalities, habits, experiences, preferences and instincts individualize people. "But methods remain the personal concern, approach, and attack of an individual, and no catalogue can ever exhaust their diversity of form and tint." Paragraph 19

But the most important aspect of method to Dewey are the traits of directness, single-mindedness (open-mindedness), whole-heartedness and responsibility. Paragraph 20

1)Directness for Dewey is probably represented these days by an engaging focus. The student is intent on inquiry on a particular interest. Distractions are limited. Paragraph 23

2)As far as open-mindedness is explained, Dewey mentions that in an educational aim there is some direction toward an assumed end, but that should not preclude other possibilities as they suggest themselves. "But intellectual growth means constant expansion of horizons and consequent formation of new purposes and new responses. These are impossible without an active disposition to welcome points of view hitherto alien; an active desire to entertain considerations which modify existing purposes." Paragraph 24

It is hard to believe that Dewey wrote this almost one hundred years ago. He starts the next paragraph this way: "Exorbitant desire for uniformity of procedure and for prompt external results are the chief foes which the open-minded attitude meets in school…. Probably the chief cause of devotion to rigidity of method is, however, that it seems to promise speedy, accurately measurable, correct results." Has it really been a hundred years? Paragraph 25

3)Single-mindedness or open-mindedness can be conveyed as "completeness of interest…. It is equivalent to mental integrity. Absorption, engrossment, full concern with subject matter for its own sake, nurture it. Divided interest and evasion destroy it." Paragraph 27

4)Responsibility is the same thing as intellectual thoroughness "seeing a thing through." Paragraph 33

Questions for application:

1. What do you think is more valuable: learning how an expert found his way to the solution, or developing a data bank of previous solutions? Why?

2. What do you think about Dewey's comment that stratifying students into exclusive classes hurts originality? How do students who are not considered bright still develop originality, and become self-actualized as learners?

3. We all need role models. Describe a student who exemplified the four essential traits of Individual Method? (Directness, open-mindedness, single-mindedness, responsibility.)

Notes and Quotes:

Chapter 14:
The Nature of Subject Matter

You may be pleased with Dewey's first sentence in this chapter. "So far as the nature of subject matter in principle is concerned, there is nothing to add to what has been said." However, this chapter has 14 pages! Paragraph 1

"Organized subject matter represents the ripe fruitage of experiences like (the instructors'), experiences involving the same world, and powers and needs similar to (students'). It does not represent perfection or infallible wisdom; but it is the best at command to further new experiences which may, in some respects at least, surpass the achievements embodied in existing knowledge and works of art." Paragraph 4

Dewey speaks of social norms passed on in primitive tribes as part of survival, physical survival and social survival. As things get more formal, teachers think their body of learning is transferable. But Dewey says "The subject matter of the learner is not, therefore, it cannot be, identical with the formulated, the crystallized, and the systematized subject matter of the adult; the material as found in books and in works of art, etc. The latter represents the possibilities of the former, not its existing state." In other words, that was their accomplished adult knowledge, but you must get your own, perhaps along the same lines. Paragraph 5

The four stages in the growth in subject matter of the learner are described this way. 1) "The knowledge which comes first to persons, and that remains most deeply ingrained, is knowledge of how to do; how to walk, talk, read, write, skate, ride a bicycle, manage a machine, calculate, drive a horse, sell goods, manage people, and so on indefinitely." Paragraph 8

2) "The place of communication in personal doing supplies us with a criterion for estimating the value of informational material in school. Does it grow naturally out of some question with which the student is concerned? Does it fit into his more direct acquaintance so as to increase its efficacy and deepen its meaning? If it meets these two requirements, it is educative." Paragraph 12

3) "Science or rationalized knowledge…represents in its degree, the perfected outcome of learning,--its consummation. What is known, in a given sense, is what is sure, certain, settled, disposed of; that which we think with rather than that which we think about. In its honorable sense, knowledge is distinguished

from opinion, guesswork, speculation, and mere tradition. In knowledge things are ascertained; they are so and not dubiously otherwise." Paragraph 18

4) "Subject Matter as Social…All information and systematized scientific subject matter have been worked out under the conditions of social life and have been transmitted by social means…. There is truth in the saying that education must first be human and only after that professional….material is humanized in the degree in which it connects with the common interests of men as men." Paragraph 24

Remember that Dewey believes that democracy is dependent on thinking people to listen to the input of other thinking people and consider ways everyone can learn from each other, and in that way advance society. You cannot have a learning environment that has no connection to a social context and you cannot advance thinking without a group to exchange ideas with. That is why the social component is always essential to Dewey.

Today we would probably say that the student has some first-hand connection with the topic. Second, that the information related to the topic is "authentic", sourced to the activity. Third, that the student is satisfied with the correctness of the conclusion. And finally we would say that pragmatism provides the value in the subject matter, so it is not just head knowledge.

Dewey believes that rote learning, canned answers, test answer preparation, and drills are as far from the intellect of the learner as automation is.

Questions for application:

1. For Dewey a teacher's knowledge is a teaching base, not a content to transfer. How does the individualization of aims capitalize on the resource of the teacher?

2. Dewey's discussion of science is not about experimentation, it is about each student validating or confirming ideas as true to their experience. If you apply this broader term to the classroom, the "Prove it!" challenge, or "Why do you think that's true?", what would your discussions look like in math, in science or even with coworkers in playground/parking lot politics?

3. The humanist, Dewey always sought the greater good before the benefit of a subgroup. In a world of individualized competition, where do your students give pause to social/societal concerns in their individual quests? How widely do they perceive their social context? Is their learning pragmatic enough to require a social context for ratification or application? Dewey says it must.

Notes and Quotes:

Chapter 15:
Play and Work in the Curriculum

"Experience has shown that when children have a chance at physical activities which bring their natural impulses into play, going to school is a joy, management is less of a burden, and learning is easier." Paragraph 1

"Doubtless the fact that children normally engage in play and work out of school has seemed to many educators a reason why they should concern themselves in school with things radically different. School time seemed too precious to spend in doing things over again what children were sure to do anyway." Paragraph 3

"It is the business of the school to set up an environment in which play and work shall be conducted with reference to facilitating desirable mental and moral growth. It is not enough just to introduce plays and games, hand work and manual exercises. Everything depends upon the way in which they are employed." Paragraph 4

"The problem of the educator is to engage pupils in these activities in such ways that while manual skill and technical efficiency are gained and immediate satisfaction found in the work, together with preparation for later usefulness, these things shall be subordinated to education—that is, to intellectual results and the forming of a socialized disposition." Early technical skills are not just foundational for future more complicated skills, but they should also already elicit issues of logic, description, mathematics and social effects. Paragraph 6

"For the person approaching a subject, the simple thing is his purpose—the use he desires to make of material, tool, or technical process, no matter how complicated the process of execution may be. The unity of the purpose, with the concentration upon details which it entails, confers simplicity upon the elements which have to be reckoned with in the course of action." Deliberate interaction with components of a process, render them familiar and simple in the way they support the unity of the purpose. No matter how complex the process, the significance of components is clearly (simply) related to the purpose. Paragraph 10

One of the dangers Dewey sees in education is that as students progress, their attention and their direction are "deflected" to profit motives. Society supports their education and he believes the students should reciprocally support society, as well as themselves. Educators are charged to make sure the broad view is evident to students. Paragraph 13

"Both (work and play) involve ends consciously entertained and the selection and adaptations of materials and processes designed to affect the desired ends. The difference between them is largely one of time-span, influencing the directness of the connection of means and ends." Paragraph 16

Dewey waxes almost metaphysically at times. When he comments on the activities which a person pursues out of intrinsic interest, he sees a smooth transition of purpose: "When fairly remote results of a definite character are foreseen and enlist persistent effort for their accomplishment, play passes into work." Paragraph 19

Dewey would have approved of the story of a stone mason who was asked why he persisted so many years laying stone for a church. He replied that we was not laying stone; he was building a cathedral. And Dewey would have then asked what was the benefit of having another cathedral, hoping to hear that society would benefit in some particular way. He felt that work which seems like drudgery can have a fulfillment if the outcome is intrinsic in the labor. The more connections with society, the more fulfilling the labor. But that requires that those who labor have a sense of wider purpose.

Questions for application

1. How would Dewey respond to the position: homogeneous groupings for skill development, heterogeneous groupings for concept development?

2. In your experience, how has either grouping resulted in play or coercion?

3. In what ways are students in your environment reminded of social obligations? How does that grow out of the ethical considerations of the content material, not merely as a service project?

4. For Dewey, play is purposeful discovery activity. If a teacher practices giving a reward of "free time" to students, how can that time be purposeful "free time" rather than idleness or fooling, as Dewey would term it?

Notes and Quotes:

Chapter 16:
The Significance of Geography and History

"There is no limit to the meaning which an action may come to possess. It all depends upon the context of perceived connections in which it is placed; the reach of imagination in realizing connections is inexhaustible." Paragraph 1

"The advantage which an activity of man has in appropriating and finding meanings makes his education something else than the manufacture of a tool or the training of an animal. The latter increase efficiency; they do not develop significance. The final educational importance of such occupations in play and work as were considered in the last chapter is that they afford the most direct instrumentalities for such extension of meaning. Set going under adequate conditions they are magnets for gathering and retaining an indefinitely wide scope of intellectual considerations. They provide vital centers for the reception and assimilation of information." Paragraph 2

"The meanings with which activities become charged, concern nature and man. This is an obvious truism, which however gains meaning when translated into educational equivalents. So translated, it signifies that geography and history supply subject matter which gives background and outlook, intellectual perspective, to what might otherwise be narrow personal actions or mere forms of technical skill." Paragraph 3

"We realize that we are citizens of no mean city in discovering the scene in space of which we are denizens, and the continuous manifestation of endeavor in time of which we are heirs and continuers. Thus our ordinary daily experiences cease to be things of the moment and gain enduring substance." Paragraph 3

Dewey's definitions of learning geography and history do not match university course catalogs or even state standards of educational goals. His is the broadest definition of man's experience with space and time. "To 'learn geography' is to gain in power to perceive the spatial, the natural, connections of an ordinary act; to 'learn history' is essentially to gain in power to recognize its human connections." Paragraph 5

"While geography emphasizes the physical side and history the social, these are only emphases in a common topic, namely, the associated life of men. For this associated life, with its experiments, its ways and means, its achievements and failures, does not go on in the sky nor yet in a vacuum. It takes place on earth. This setting of nature does not bear to social activities the relation that the scenery of a theatrical performance bears to a dramatic representation; it enters into the very make-up of the social happenings that form history." Paragraph 7

You don't want to be imaginatively inert, do you? "The earth as the home of man is humanizing and unified; the earth viewed as a miscellany of facts is scattering and imaginatively inert. Geography is a topic that originally appeals to imagination—even to the romantic imagination. It shares in the wonder and glory that attach to adventure, travel, and exploration." Paragraph 9

Ready for another loop phrase? "History deals with the past, but this past is the history of the present…. The true starting point of history is always some present situation with its problems." Old information has no significance unless it relates to the present. Paragraph 12

"Perhaps the most neglected branch of history in general education is intellectual history. We are only just beginning to realize that the great heroes who have advanced human destiny are not its politicians, generals, and diplomatists, but the scientific discoverers and inventors who have put into mans hands the instrumentalities of an expanding and controlled experience, and the artists and poets who have celebrated his struggles, triumphs, and defeats in such language, pictorial, plastic, or written, that their meaning is rendered universally accessible to others." Paragraph 18

Questions for application

1. Dewey contrasts "imaginatively inexhaustible" and "imaginatively inert." Describe a situation in your world where each is evident.

2. "Through manifestation of endeavor we gain enduring substance." How would you explain this to your students?

3. Dewey wants contributions to the associated life of men, not meaningless activity. Looking back at the quote from paragraph 7, would he agree with Shakespeare that we are all actors upon a stage?

Notes and Quotes:

education must be put into a relatable
context to have meaning.

Chapter 17:
Science in the Course of Study

"By science is meant, as already stated, that knowledge which is the outcome of methods of observation, reflection, and testing which are deliberately adopted to secure a settled, assured subject matter. It involves an intelligent and persistent endeavor to revise current beliefs so as to weed out what is erroneous, to add to their accuracy, and above all, to give them such shape that the dependencies of the various facts upon one another may be as obvious as possible.... Both logically and educationally, science is the perfecting of knowing, its last stage." Paragraph 1

Dewey accuses educators of teaching science and math without experiential components. He acknowledges that symbols can readily be learned by students as representations for items and processes. But he chafes about whether knowing formulae, definitions and rules constitute useful learning. "No one would have a knowledge of a machine who could enumerate all the materials entering into its structure, but only he who knew their uses and could tell why they are employed as they are." Paragraph 9

Doubtless, Dewey would disapprove of the predominant method today of teaching math algorithms in advance of the word problems. And with his pragmatic approach to instruction, he would be in dismay that many marginal students never get to the application word problems, exacerbating their struggle. Even students who do perform the tasks to solve the word problems are taught to do it simply in order to practice the algorithm, rather than face a problem and select the appropriate algorithm. That is parallel to the last sentence in the previous paragraph. Much of American math education is upside-down.

He makes a rather utopian statement. "Science has familiarized men with the idea of development, taking effect practically in persistent gradual amelioration of the estate of our common humanity." He sees science as keeping people real, advancing industrialization, and as of yet immature in the sense of perspective and social responsibility. He perceived the possibilities of atrocities being performed in the name of science when scientific work is isolated from the general social milieu. Paragraph 13

For Dewey the term empirical knowledge means factual, accumulated and unprocessed. It has not been reasoned and does not allow for creative inferences. "Experimental science means the possibility of using past experiences as the servant, not the master, of mind. It means that reason operates within experience, not beyond it, to give it an intelligent or reasonable quality. Science is experience becoming rational. The effect of science is thus to change men's idea of the nature and inherent possibilities of experience. By the same token, it changes the idea and the operation of reason. Instead of being something beyond experience, remote, aloof, concerned with a sublime region that has nothing to do with the experienced facts of life, it is found indigenous in experience:--the factor by which past experiences are purified and rendered into tools for discovery and advance." Paragraph 14

You may have a table of values, or a database of clinical time-trials, but you do not have science until someone has made reasonable sense of it, implicated how it works in the real world, shown how it is an advance from pre-existing knowledge, reflected on how it relates to the greater society, and described how it propels research into greater investments in inquiry.

What is the artery of intelligence? Abstraction. We think of abstract as something representational and hard to grasp. For Dewey it is more like an ability to select significance from a situation. "For abstraction deliberately selects from the subject matter of former experiences that which is thought helpful in dealing with the new. It signifies conscious transfer of a meaning embedded in past experience for use in a new one. It is the very artery of intelligence, of the intentional rendering of one experience available for guidance of another." We may think of it as a useful reference, active in the process of synthesis, so reach a new conclusion. Paragraph 15

"Abstraction and the use of terms to record what is abstracted put the net value of individual experience at the permanent disposal of mankind." Paragraph 16

"Generalization is the counterpart of abstraction. It is the functioning of an abstraction in its application to a new concrete experience,--its extension to clarify and direct new situations. Reference to these possible applications is necessary in order that the abstraction may be fruitful, instead of a barren formalism ending in itself. Generalization is essentially a social device." Paragraph 17

Abstraction plucks the essentials from one situation to get a new, unique insight, and generalization applies the same essentials to a potentially broad array of situations. It is generalization that makes science expansive to the culture, and is therefore at the permanent disposal of mankind, and that availability renders it a social device.

"Knowledge is humanistic in quality not because it is about human products of the past, but because of what it does in liberating human intelligence and human sympathy. Any subject matter which accomplishes this result is humane, and any subject matter which does not accomplish it is not even educational." If a learning situation does not expand personal connections, it does not make the grade as something educational. Paragraph 22

Dewey concludes the chapter with this sentence. "Thus ultimately and philosophically science is the organ of general social progress." Paragraph 23

Questions for application:

1. In paragraph 1, Dewey says that science (in the wider definition of confirming beliefs) is the perfecting of knowing, its last stage. How would you describe the process leading to and undergoing the last stage?

2. In paragraph 9 Dewey discusses the difference of knowing the parts and knowing the functions of the parts. A reference was made to mathematics instruction. Where else in your learning environment do you see this difference?

3. Consider an average science class lesson. How much time is allowed for discussion of social implications of the results? Describe how that might look.

4. Knowledge is educational only when it liberates human intelligence and human sympathy, according to Dewey. Explain what you believe he means by "liberates".

Notes and Quotes:

Chapter 18:
Educational Values

"Every step from savagery to civilization is dependent upon the invention of media which enlarge the range of purely immediate experience and give it deepened as well as wider meaning by connecting it with things which can only be signified or symbolized. It is doubtless this fact which is the cause of the disposition to identify an uncultivated person with an illiterate person—so dependent are we on letters for effective representative or indirect experience." Media here means the transmission of second-hand information, usually written information. That is why an uncultivated person is considered also an illiterate person. It is media which brings us other information and enlarges our small experiential world to a broader base. Paragraph 2

Dewey warns about "the tendency to assume that pupils have a foundation of direct realization of situations efficient for the superstructure of representative experience erected by formulated school studies. This is not simply a matter of quantity or bulk. Sufficient direct experience is even more a matter of quality." Paragraph 4

These days we say you should teach for content, not coverage. Finishing the book by the end of the year whether the students have kept up or not is fruitless. It is quality of experience that counts in order to accomplish learning.

"As regards the primary school activities, it is to be borne in mind that the fundamental intent is not to amuse nor to convey information with a minimum of vexation nor yet to acquire skill,--though these results may accrue as by-products,--but to enlarge and enrich the scope of experience, and to keep alert and effective the interest in intellectual progress." The fundamental intent is to cause students to want to learn more. Paragraph 5

"A youth who has had repeated experience of the full meaning of the value of kindliness toward others built into his disposition has a measure of the worth of generous treatment of others. Without this vital appreciation, the duty and virtue of unselfishness impressed upon him by others as a standard remains purely a matter of symbols which he cannot adequately translate into realities. His 'knowledge' is second-handed; it is only a knowledge that others prize unselfishness as an excellence, and esteem him in the degree in which he exhibits it. Thus there grows up a split between a person's professed standards and his actual ones." Here the word appreciation means familiarity and a positive regard. Paragraph 9

This means that much of character education today is getting students to live up to other people's expectations, rather than acting out of their own experiences, as their own character traits. This leads to the questions as to whether students' actions are genuine or hypocritical.

"The imagination is the medium of appreciation in every field. The engagement of the imagination is the only thing that makes any activity more than mechanical." Dewey laments that many people prize mechanical type accomplishments. He feels that the imagination is able to take into account the geography of the situation. More valuable individual events have variance fostered by imagination, the "warm and intimate taking in of the full scope of a situation." Paragraph 10

"Certain conclusions follow with respect to educational values. We cannot establish a hierarchy of values among studies. It is futile to attempt to arrange them in an order, beginning with one having least worth and going on to that of maximum value. In so far as any study has a unique or irreplaceable function in experience, in so far as it marks a characteristic enrichment of life, its worth is intrinsic or incomparable. Since education is not a means to living, but is identical with the operation of living a life which is fruitful and inherently significant, the only ultimate value which can be set up is just the process of living itself." Paragraph 16

Everything you study is of practical or potential value. The purpose of education is to enrich life. The value of expanding your education is the same value as you value your life.

"This brings us to the matter of instrumental values—topics studied because of some end beyond themselves….. In general what is desirable is that a topic be presented in such a way that it either has an immediate value, and requires no justification, or else be perceived to be a means of achieving something of intrinsic value. An instrumental value then has the intrinsic value of being a means to an end." You want a child to say, "This is a great idea! I'm going to want to remember this!" Paragraph 21

To counter the departmentalization of schools, Dewey lists value criteria of schools this way. "No classification can have other than a provisional validity. The following may prove of some help. We may say that the kind of experience to which the work of the schools should contribute is one marked by executive competency in the management of resources and obstacles encountered (efficiency); by sociability, or interest in the direct companionship of others; by aesthetic taste or capacity to appreciate artistic excellence in at least some of its classic forms; by trained intellectual method, or interest in some mode of scientific achievement; and by sensitiveness to the rights and claims of others—conscientiousness. And while these considerations are not standards of value, they are useful criteria for survey, criticism, and better organization of existing methods and subject matter of instruction." Paragraph 24

Those value criteria for schools were (1) executive mastery in the management of resources and obstacles encountered; (2) interest in direct companionship of others; (3) appreciation of artistic excellence; (4) trained intellectual method of reasoning; (5) conscientiously sensitive to the rights and claims of others.

In other words, can you do the process of learning in an efficient manner, working well with others, producing high quality work, getting to significant factual results, without damaging anyone?

Questions for application

1. If you are to enlarge and enrich a scope of action and learn all kinds of related relationships of that action, which State Standard are you teaching? Think of a multi-disciplinary activity in your learning environment and list the sets of standards which may be been addressed in that process. Do any state standards match any Dewey standards?

2. Dewey believes that "generous treatment" instills a character value or trait. (Citation from Paragraph 9) How does current character education measure when a student has received "generous treatment"?

3. A common goal is to develop life-long learners. If the value of living is the value of learning, how do you get a low-motivation student to sense that learning is as crucial as living?

4. An instrumental value will get you where you want to go. Cite examples of effective instrumental value you have encountered in the last week.

Notes and Quotes:

Chapter 19:
Labor and Leisure

Since the classical time of the Greeks, liberal studies were intended for the ruling class and industrial studies for the laboring class. Each class had different educational needs. Of course the laboring class had to support both groups. Dewey cites Aristotle as clearly differentiating the needs of education between the classes. The upper class was taught to appreciate fine art, not to make it. Paragraph 2

At the time of the classical Greeks there were separations of the labor group from the leisure group. "Hence slaves, artisans and women are employed in furnishing the means of subsistence in order that others, those adequately equipped with intelligence, may live the life of leisurely concern with things intrinsically worthwhile." Paragraph 6

Dewey believes that is when and that is why education takes the two tracks. "To these two modes of occupation, with their distinction of servile and free activities (or 'arts') correspond two types of education: the base or mechanical and the liberal or intellectual." Paragraph 7

"But in spite of these changes, in spite of the abolition of legal serfdom, and the spread of democracy, with the extension of science and general education…there remains enough of a cleavage of society into a learned and an unlearned class, a leisure and a laboring class, to make (Aristotle's) point of view a most enlightening one from which to criticize the separation between culture and utility in present education." Paragraph 9

"A thorough adoption of the idea of utility would have led to instruction which tied up the studies to situations in which they were directly needed and where they were rendered immediately and not remotely helpful. It would be hard to find a subject in the curriculum within which there are not found evil results of a compromise between the two ideals. Natural science is recommended on the ground of its practical utility, but is taught as a special accomplishment in removal from application. On the other hand, music and literature are theoretically justified on the ground of their culture value and are then taught with chief emphasis upon forming technical modes of skill." Paragraph 13

The previous paragraph cited the problem when the purpose is not being matched to method. Dewey hopes for a blend. "If we had less compromise and resulting confusion, if we analyzed more carefully the respective meanings of culture and utility, we might find it easier to construct a course of study which should be useful and liberal at the same time…. It was natural for Plato to deprecate the learning of geometry and arithmetic for practical ends, because as matter of fact the practical uses to which they were put were few, lacking in content and mostly mercenary in quality. But as their social uses have increased and enlarged, their liberalizing or "intellectual" value and their practical value approach the same limit." Paragraph 14

"Nevertheless, there is already an opportunity for an education which, keeping in mind the larger features of work, will reconcile liberal nurture with training in social serviceableness, with ability to share efficiently and happily in occupations which are productive. And such an education will of itself tend to do away with the evils of the existing economic situation. In the degree in which men have an active concern in the ends that control their activity, their activity becomes free or voluntary and loses its externally enforced and servile quality, even though the physical aspect of behavior remain the same. In what is termed politics, democratic social organization makes provision for this direct participation in control: in the economic region, control remains external and autocratic. Hence the split between inner mental action and outer physical action of which the traditional distinction between the liberal and the utilitarian is the reflex. An education which should unify the disposition of the members of society would do much to unify society itself." Paragraph 16

First look back at what he says about the same behaviors of employment. If you are doing your work out of obligation it is serfdom. If you do it because you have chosen that activity voluntarily, you are free. But that only addresses the dualism discussed in this chapter. Looking back at previous chapters, Dewey still expects that voluntary choice of activity to have stemmed from pursuing individual interests in intellectual growth, lifelong learning, social awareness and social contribution. He looks for scholarly tradesmen and handy intellectuals.

His last sentence of the chapter is this. "The problem of education in a democratic society is to do away with the dualism and to construct a course of studies which makes thought a guide of free practice for all and which makes leisure a reward of accepting responsibility for service, rather than a state of exemption from it." Paragraph 17

Questions for application:

1. Identify dichotomies in our culture that mirror the leisure vs. labor concept.

2. To what extent are there systems in place to support the dichotomies identified?

3. To what extent can or has education been able to "modify the disposition" of society? This is the reciprocal to Dewey's statement that the expression of educational structure is a reflection of the values of that society.

4. In the current backlash about freedom from general education mandatory classes (liberal arts) and moving toward trade school (career education) structures, how do we keep a blend of social responsibility with technical artistry?

Notes and Quotes:

Chapter 20:
Intellectual and Practical Studies

In discussing knowing and doing, Dewey returns to his reference to Plato and Aristotle. "Again, experience always involved lack, need, desire; it was never self-sufficing. Rational knowing, on the other hand, was complete and comprehensive within itself. Hence the practical life was in a condition of perpetual flux, while the intellectual knowledge concerned eternal truth." Paragraph 2

If Dewey calls you an empiric, you have not been complimented. He regards you as a lab technician who performs routine duties, without knowing how it works or why it is needed. Certainly an empiric would not consider ethics.

Once again Dewey forms the meaning of "empirical" around repetitive trials, which are unrelated to rational reflection. "Just because of the lack of science or reason in "experience" it is hard to keep it at its poor best. The empiric easily degenerates into the quack. He does not know where his knowledge begins or leaves off, and so when he gets beyond routine conditions he begins to pretend—to make claims for which there is no justification, and to trust to luck and to ability to impose upon others—to 'bluff'. Moreover, he assumes that because he has learned one thing, he knows others—as the history of Athens showed that common craftsmen thought they could manage household affairs, education, and politics, because they had learned to do the specific things of their trades. Experience is always hovering, then, on the edge of pretense, of sham, of seeing, and appearance, in distinction from the reality upon which reason lays hold." Consider the examples of celebrities making public comments about politics or medical claims. Paragraph 6

There is at least one consulting service that addresses the tendency to perform beyond competence. This service asks medical students to describe the extent of their personal knowledge in sub-topic areas. The students are then told that what they have produced is actually a map of the boundaries of their ignorance. To go into unknown territory is un-professional.

Dewey cites Bacon as one of the individuals who changed the concept of knowledge during the seventeenth and eighteenth centuries. "In general, it presents us with an almost complete reversal of the classic doctrine of the relations of experience and reason. To Plato experience meant habituation, or the conservation of the net product of a lot of past chance trials. Reason meant the principle of reform, of progress, of increase of control. Devotion to the cause of reason meant breaking through the limitations of custom and getting at things as they really were. To the modern reformers, the situation was the other way around. Reason, universal principles, a priori notions, meant either blank forms which had to be filled in by experience, by sense observations, in order to get significance and validity; or else were mere indurated prejudices, dogmas imposed by authority, which masqueraded and found protection under august names.... It meant openness to new impressions; eagerness in discovery and invention instead of absorption in tabulations and systematizing received ideas and 'proving' them by means of the relations they sustained to one another." Paragraph 11

To over simplify (something Dewey almost never does), the Greeks seemed to use reason to understand, classify, and synthesize knowledge, and have appreciation of the arts, at least among the leisure class. The change cited in the previous paragraph seems to include all of that, but also to take reasoning as something that is an intellectual construction, not just an intellectual task.

"The change was twofold. Experience lost the practical meaning which it had borne from the time of Plato. It ceased to mean ways of doing and being done to, and became a name for something intellectual and cognitive. It meant the appreciation of material which should ballast and check the exercise of reasoning.... In the second place, the interest in experience as a means of basing truth upon objects, upon nature, led to looking at the mind as purely receptive." Paragraph 12

John Locke used the term 'blank slate' to signify the complete openness of the brain to input. Helvetius, another significant person of the time, was the chief thinker among a position known as "sensationalists". "If knowledge comes from the impressions made upon us by natural objects, it is impossible to procure knowledge without the use of objects which impress the mind. Words, like all kinds of linguistic symbols, in the lack of prior presentations of objects with which they may be associated, convey nothing but sensations of their own shape and color—certainly not a very instructive kind of knowledge." Paragraph 14

This movement from classical thinking to a more contemporary thinking was much more appropriate to industrialization. "Sense perceptions were indeed indispensable, but there was less reliance upon sense perceptions in their natural or customary form than in the older science. They were no longer regarded as containing within themselves some "form" or "species" of universal kind in a disguised mask of sense which could be stripped off by rational thought. On the contrary, the first thing was to alter and extend the data of sense perception: to act upon the given objects of sense by the lens of the telescope and microscope, and by all sorts of experimental devices. To accomplish this in a way which would arouse new ideas required even more general ideas than were at the command of ancient science. But these general conceptions were no longer taken to give knowledge in themselves. They were implements for instituting, conducting, interpreting experimental inquiries and formulating their results." Paragraph 21

"The logical outcome is a new philosophy of experience and knowledge, a philosophy which no longer puts experience in opposition to rational knowledge and explanation. Experience is no longer a mere summarizing of what has been done in a more or less chance way in the past; it is a deliberate control of what is done with reference to making what happens to us and what we do to things as fertile as possible of suggestions and a means for trying out the validity of the suggestions." Paragraph 22

The contemporary thinking for Dewey, at his time, is more expansive. Instead of drilling down to the smallest entity of a subject, science validates a trait and expands to see how many more ways that trait can be suggested and validated. That is the same growth pattern Dewey has for learners. The learner, and also science, should always be expanding on core knowledge.

Questions for application:

1. Consider the commercials for weight loss, hair regrowth, or other body enhancements. To what degree is there scientific validation and at what point can one perceive a "bluff" happens? We teach students to recognize fact vs. fiction. But where do we teach them that a line of facts can transition into a line of fiction? If we have done so effectively, why are those commercials so prevalent?

2. Describe how a curriculum based on the concept of "tabula rasa" or "clean slate" would look in your educational environment.

3. Since his book came out in 1916 there has been exponential growth in technological advances. Doctors had just learned of the importance of washing their hands between patients back then. But in some cases rapid growth in technology cannot be synonymous with sweeping growth. As recently as 1992 the New England Journal of Medicine did an observational study in an intensive care unit, and recorded that there was no more than 48% compliance with the hand washing rule. Dewey says knowledge, not applied, is wasted. The demand for implementation of research based curriculums is common, but describe the instructional practices you are aware of that are still used in spite of research proven improvements and alternatives.

Notes and Quotes:

Chapter 21:
Physical and Social Studies:
Naturalism and Humanism

Dewey reminds us that the Greeks wanted to control nature. After them came the Romans who wanted to control people. Then he describes the term Scholasticism.

"Scholasticism frequently has been used since the time of the revival of learning as a term for reproach. But all that it means is a method of The Schools, or of the School Men. In its essence, it is nothing but a highly effective systematization of the methods of teaching and learning which are appropriate to transmit an authoritative body of truths. Where literature rather than contemporary nature and society furnishes material of study, methods must be adapted to defining, expounding, and interpreting the received material, rather than to inquiry, discovery, and invention. And at bottom what is called Scholasticism is the whole-hearted and consistent formulation and application of the methods which are suited to instruction when the material of instruction is taken ready made, rather than as something which students are to find out for themselves. So far as schools still teach from textbooks and rely upon the principle of authority and acquisition rather than upon that of discovery and inquiry, their methods are Scholastic—minus the logical accuracy and system of Scholasticism at its best." It is second hand learning, passing on learning from a source more like literature, rather than as experience. Paragraph 7

After revisiting the fifteenth century and its "renascence" reject the supernatural, Dewey notes that the sixteenth century science went back to a Greek view. Finally he arrives at "The Present Educational Problem".

"In truth, experience knows no division between human concerns and a purely mechanical physical world. Man's home is nature; his purposes and aims are dependent for execution upon natural conditions. Separated from such conditions they become empty dreams and idle indulgences of fancy. From the standpoint of human experience, and hence of educational endeavor, any distinction which can be justly made between nature and man is a distinction between the conditions which have to be reckoned with in the formation and execution of our practical aims, and the aims themselves." Paragraph 17

"Every step forward in the social sciences—the studies termed history, economics, politics, sociology—shows that social questions are capable of being intelligently coped with only in the degree in which we employ the method of collected data, forming hypotheses, and testing them in action which is characteristic of natural science, and in the degree in which we utilize in behalf of the promotion of social welfare the technical knowledge ascertained by physics and chemistry. Advanced methods of dealing with such perplexing problems as insanity, intemperance, poverty, public sanitation, city planning and conservation of natural resources, the constructive use of governmental agencies for furthering the public good without weakening personal initiative, all illustrate the direct dependence of our important social concerns upon the methods and results of natural science." Paragraph 17

In Dewey's mind there is no way for the intellect to avoid contact with the physical world. He also believes in social experimentation to address society's ills. But the experimentation must be methodical, not biased by a tradition or a casual path.

"With respect then to both humanistic and naturalistic studies, education should take its departure from this close interdependence. It should aim not at keeping science as a study of nature apart from literature as a record of human interests, but at cross-fertilizing both the natural sciences and the various human disciplines such as history, literature, economics, and politics." Paragraph 18

"Not only does the business occupation of their parents depend upon scientific applications, but household pursuits, the maintenance of health, the sights seen upon the streets, embody scientific achievements and stimulate interest in the connected scientific principles. The obvious pedagogical starting point of scientific instruction is not to teach things labeled science, but to utilize the familiar occupations and appliances to direct observation and experiment, until pupils have arrived at a knowledge of some fundamental principles by understanding them in their familiar practical workings." Paragraph 20

"As a matter of fact, any subject is cultural in the degree in which it is apprehended in its widest possible range of meanings. Perception of meanings depends upon perception of connections, of context. To see a scientific fact or law in its human as well as in its physical and technical context is to enlarge its significance and give it increased cultural value." Paragraph 21

"In short, when we consider the close connection between literary and aesthetic cultivation and an aristocratic social organization on the other, we get light on the opposition between technical scientific studies and refining literary studies. We have before us the need of overcoming this separation in education if society is to be truly democratic." Democracy demands interplay of diverse subject areas as well as of diverse individuals. Paragraph 25

Questions for application

1. If you take the science steps of hypothesis, testing, analysis, conclusion, how would that apply to the study of a book? How would that apply to the study of contemporary political preferences? Dating?

2. Describe whether the environmentalist "green" approach combines the interests of science and humanity.

3. There is a television series called "Follow that Food" which tracks a familiar food item from farmer to processor to retailer to consumer. How might a similar series on the fruitfulness of scientific discoveries develop? Describe the first show from start to finish.

Notes and Quotes:

Chapter 22:
The Individual and the World

Dewey comments on the religious individualism of the Middle Ages. "The deepest concern of life was the salvation of the individual soul. In the later Middle Ages, this latent individualism found conscious formulation in the nominalistic philosophies, which treated the structure of knowledge as something built up within the individual, through his own acts and mental states.... The reaction against authority in all spheres of life, and the intensity of the struggle, against great odds, for freedom of action and inquiry, led to such an emphasis upon personal observations and ideas as in effect to isolate mind, and set it apart from the world to be known." Paragraph 3

"This isolation is reflected in the great development of that branch of philosophy known as epistemology—the theory of knowledge. The identification of mind with the self, and the setting up of the self as something independent and self-sufficient, created such a gulf between the knowing mind and the world that it became a question how knowledge was possible at all.... In short, practical individualism, or struggle for greater freedom of thought in action, was translated into philosophic subjectivism." Paragraph 4

Some change is inevitable.
"Moral philosophies which have started from such premises have developed four typical ways of dealing with the question. (i) One method represents the survival of the older authoritative position, with such concessions and compromises as the progress of events has made absolutely inevitable." Paragraph 13

Come reason together
"(ii) Another method is sometimes termed rationalism or abstract intellectualism.... It was a powerful factor in the negative and dissolving criticism of doctrines having nothing but tradition and class interest behind them; it accustomed men to freedom of discussion and the notion that beliefs had to be submitted to criteria of reasonableness." Paragraph 14

Mind your own intellect
"(iii) While this rationalistic philosophy was developing in France, English thought appealed to the intelligent self-interest of individuals in order to secure outer unity in the acts which issued from isolated streams of consciousness.... Education was to instill in individuals a sense that non-interference with others and some degree of positive regard for their welfare were necessary for security in the pursuit of one's own happiness." Paragraph 15

Synthesis of dualism, but only in philosophy
"(iv) Typical German philosophy followed another path. It started from what was essentially the rationalistic philosophy of Descartes and his French successors…. German thought (as in Hegel) made a synthesis of the two. Reason is absolute. Nature is incarnate reason. History is reason in its progressive unfolding in man. An individual becomes rational only as he absorbs into himself the content of rationality in nature and in social institutions…. It made for efficiency of organization more than did any of the types of philosophy previously mentioned, but it made no provision for free experimental modification of this organization. Political democracy, with its belief in the right of the individual desire and purpose to take part in readapting even the fundamental constitution of society, was foreign to it." Paragraph 16
That the German philosophy probably did not address political democracy was probably obvious since Dewey put this book together at the time of the First World War when the Prussian leadership was so strong.

Freedom involves all tasks and institutions for Dewey
"But the essence of the demand for freedom is the need of conditions which will enable an individual to make his own special contribution to a group interest, and to partake of its activities in such ways that social guidance shall be a matter of his own mental attitude, and not a mere authoritative dictation of his acts. Because what is often called discipline and 'government' has to do with the external side of conduct alone, a similar meaning is attached, by reaction, to freedom. But when it is perceived that each idea signifies the quality of mind expressed in action, the supposed opposition between them falls away. Freedom means essentially the part played by thinking—which is personal—in learning; --it means intellectual initiative, independence in observation, judicious invention, foresight of consequences, and ingenuity of adaptation to them." Paragraph 18

Like the German approach synthesizing the application of mind and action, Dewey adds the democratic mandate of opportunity to transform or reorganize society through the richness of diverse entities affecting others and being, in turn, moved by them.

Questions for application

1. If freedom needs conditions to allow individual contribution, how can learning environments be structured or phrased to invite students to make suggestions on improving conditions for social organization?

2. Although it may not have been intended to be sequential, fill in the outline of a project lesson plan suggested in the last sentence quoted:

Intellectual initiative

Independence in observation

Judicious invention

Foresight of consequences

Ingenuity of adaptation

Notes and Quotes:

Chapter 23:
Vocational Aspects of Education

Dewey starts with a definition. "It is necessary to define the meaning of vocation with some fullness in order to avoid the impression that an education which centers about it is narrowly practical, if not merely pecuniary. A vocation means nothing but such a direction of life activities as renders them perceptibly significant to a person, because of the consequences they accomplish, and also useful to his associates. The opposite of a career is neither leisure nor culture, but aimlessness, capriciousness, the absence of cumulative achievement in experience, on the personal side, and idle display, parasitic dependence upon the others, on the social side." A non-career life is of no individual significance and of no social benefit. Paragraph 2

"We must avoid not only limitation of conception of vocation to the occupations where immediately tangible commodities are produced, but also the notion that vocations are distributed in an exclusive way, one and only one to each person." Paragraph 2

"A person must have experience, he must live, if his artistry is to be more than a technical accomplishment. He cannot find the subject matter of his artistic activity within his art; this must be an expression of what he suffers and enjoys in other relationships—a thing which depends in turn upon the alertness and sympathy of his interests…. Hence it is not the business of education to foster this tendency (toward specialization), but rather to safeguard against it, so that the scientific inquirer shall not be merely the scientist, the teacher merely the pedagogue, the clergyman merely one who wears the cloth, and so on." Paragraph 4

Dewey returns to his concept of educational aims. "An occupation is the only thing which balances the distinctive capacity of an individual with his social service. To find out what one is fitted to do and to secure an opportunity to do it is the key to happiness…. With reference to other members of a community, this adequacy of action signifies, of course, that they are getting the best service the person can render." Paragraph 5

"An occupation is a continuous activity having a purpose. Education through occupations consequently combines within itself more of the factors conducive to learning than any other method. It calls instincts and habits into play; it is a foe to passive receptivity. It has an end in view; results are to be accomplished. Hence it appeals to thought; it demands that an idea of an end be steadily maintained, so that activity cannot be either routine or capricious. Since the movement of activity must be progressive, leading from one state to another, observation and ingenuity are required at each stage to overcome obstacles and to discover and readapt means of execution." Paragraph 6

"A calling is also of necessity an organizing principle for information and ideas; for knowledge and intellectual growth. It provides an axis which runs through an immense diversity of detail; it causes different experiences, facts, items of information to fall into order with one another." Paragraph 7

"Even if adults have to be on the lookout to see that their calling does not shut down on them and fossilize them, educators must certainly be careful that the vocational preparation of youth is such as to engage them in a continuous reorganization of aims and methods." Paragraph 9

"The problem is not that of making the schools an adjunct to manufacture and commerce, but of utilizing the factors of industry to make school life more active, more full of immediate meaning, more connected with out-of-school experience." Is this in your school or district mission statement? Paragraph 19

Here is Dewey's ideal of a vocational view of education. "It signifies a society in which every person shall be occupied in something which makes the lives of others better worth living, and which accordingly makes the ties which bind persons together more perceptible—which breaks down the barriers of distance between them. It denotes a state of affairs in which the interest of each in his work is uncoerced and intelligent; based upon its congeniality to his own aptitudes.... No insuperable obstacles, given the intelligent will for its realization, stand in the way." Paragraph 20

"Sentimentally, it may seem harsh to say that the greatest evil of the present regime is not found in poverty and in the suffering which it entails, but in the fact that so many persons have callings which make no appeal to them, which are pursued simply for the money reward that accrues. For such callings constantly provoke one to aversion, ill will, and a desire to slight and evade. Neither men's hearts not their minds are in their work." Paragraph 22

The opposition of industrial interests to thoughtful training is "the presage of a more equitable and enlightened social order, for it gives evidence of the dependence of social reorganization upon educational reconstruction. It is accordingly an encouragement to those believing in a better order to undertake the promotion of a vocational education which does not subject youth to the demands and standards of the present system, but which utilizes its scientific and social factors to develop a courageous intelligence, and to make intelligence practical and executive." Paragraph 25

Questions for application

1. From the text it appears that even in the early 1900's of John Dewey there was a sense that an employee of 40 years in the same company might have had more than one career. List careers which have come to be and gone away during the ensuing 90 years.

2. How does ingenuity in an individual career apply to professional development as companies reinvent themselves to stay current with a changing marketplace? To what extent have teachers reinvented themselves and reorganized schooling?

3. How can factors of manufacture and commerce help make school life more active and be more transcending to the school location?

4. If someone is in a career where they have no heart and no desire to actually perform, can an occupational counselor guide them to a meaningful commitment or must they follow their heart's leading to a new career path? Do you agree that to remain professionally unsatisfied is worse than poverty? Do you currently work primarily for satisfaction or for money?

5. Based on the last line of text in this chapter, describe an intelligence that is "courageous, practical and executive". How is that developed?

Notes and Quotes:

Chapter 24:
Philosophy of Education

"Our further task is to extract and make explicit the idea of philosophy implicit in these considerations. We have already virtually described, though not defined, philosophy in terms of the problems with which it deals; and we have pointed out that these problems originate in the conflicts and difficulties of social life. The problems are such things as the relations of mind and matter; body and soul; humanity and physical nature; the individual and the social; theory—or knowing, and practice—or doing. The philosophical systems which formulate these problems record the main lineaments and difficulties of contemporary practice. They bring to explicit consciousness what men have come to think, in virtue of the quality of their current experience, about nature, themselves, and the reality they conceive to include or to govern." Paragraph 6

"On the side of the attitude of the philosopher and of those who accept his conclusions, there is the endeavor to attain as unified, consistent, and complete an outlook upon experience as is possible. This aspect is expressed in the word 'philosophy'—love of wisdom. Whenever philosophy has been taken seriously, it has always been assumed that it signified achieving a wisdom which would influence the conduct of life." Paragraph 7

"It is of assistance to connect philosophy with thinking in its distinction from knowledge. Knowledge, grounded knowledge, is science; it represents objects which have been settled, ordered, disposed of rationally. Thinking, on the other hand, is prospective in reference. It is occasioned by an unsettlement and it aims at overcoming a disturbance. Philosophy is thinking what the known demands of us—what responsive attitude it exacts. It is an idea of what is possible, not a record of accomplished fact. Hence it is hypothetical, like all thinking. It presents an assignment of something to be done—something to be tried. Its value lies not in furnishing solutions (which can be achieved only in action) but in defining difficulties and suggesting methods for dealing with them. Philosophy might almost be described as thinking which has become conscious of itself—which has generalized its place, function and value in experience." We might say that he refers to metacognition, thinking about thinking. Here, he refers to thinking about clarifying questions and surveying potential methods. Paragraph 11

"The fact that philosophic problems arise because of widespread and widely felt difficulties in social practice is disguised because philosophers become a specialized class which uses technical language, unlike the vocabulary in which the direct difficulties are stated. But where a system becomes influential, its connection with a conflict of interest calling for some program of social adjustment may always be discovered. At this point the intimate connection between philosophy and education appears. In fact, education offers a vantage ground from which to penetrate to the human, as distinct from the technical, significance of philosophic discussions. The student of philosophy 'in itself' is always in danger of taking it as so much nimble or severe intellectual exercise— as something said by philosophers and concerning them alone. But when philosophic issues are approached from the side of the kind of mental disposition to which they correspond, or the differences in educational practice they make when acted upon, the life-situations which they formulate can never be far from view. If a theory makes no difference in educational endeavor, it must be artificial. The educational point of view enables one to envisage the philosophic problems where they arise and thrive, where they are at home, and where acceptance or rejection makes a difference in practice." Paragraph 14

For Dewey everything must find application to be of value. He was president of the American Philosophical Society and yet he says that philosophy is just word play unless it can be put into practice. "If we are willing to conceive education as the process of forming fundamental disposition, intellectual and emotional, toward nature and fellow men, philosophy may even be defined as the general theory of education…. Business and schooling tends to become a routine empirical affair unless its aims and methods are animated by such a broad and sympathetic survey of its place in contemporary life as it is in the business of philosophy to provide." Paragraph 15

"Philosophy thus has a double task: that of criticizing existing aims with respect to the existing state of science, pointing out values which have become obsolete with the command of new resources, showing what values are merely sentimental because there are no means for their realization; and also that of interpreting the results of specialized science in their bearing on future social endeavor. It is impossible that it should have any success in these tasks without educational equivalents as to what to do and what not to do…. Education is the laboratory in which philosophic distinctions become concrete and are tested." That's a weighty role for education to play. Paragraph 16

"The reconstruction of philosophy, of education, and of social ideals and methods thus go hand in hand. If there is especial need of educational reconstruction at the present time, if this need makes urgent a reconsideration of the basic ideas of traditional philosophic systems, it is because of the thoroughgoing change in social life accompanying the advance in science, the industrial revolution, and the development of democracy. Such practical changes cannot take place without demanding an educational reformation to meet them, and without leading men to ask what ideas and ideals are implicit in these social changes, and what revisions they require of the ideas and ideals which are inherited from older and unlike cultures." Paragraph 21

If the swift evolution of technology in the early 1900's caused Dewey and his contemporaries to that consider educational philosophy should allow radical reformation, how much of that happened, and how much more reformation of education is happening today due to our advanced level of technology?

Questions for application

1. Tenets of belief are statements everyone can agree to as attitudes about a situation, such as "All children can learn". What sort of educational/philosophical process do you think would need to take place in your organization to move from a statement like "All children can learn" to "All children will read at grade level by the end of grade 3"? Or is the second statement just an "aim"?

2. To what extent do you feel that education is "animated by such a broad and sympathetic survey of its place in contemporary life"?

3. In what ways is your classroom, or might your classroom become, the laboratory in which philosophic distinctions become concrete and are tested, the ideas and ideals of a changing culture?

Notes and Quotes:

Chapter 25:
Theories of Knowledge

Dewey believes that all the dualism of the philosophical systems of the past "culminate in one between knowing and doing, theory and practice, between mind as the end and spirit of action and the body as its organ and means.... We shall be content to summarize the forces which tend to make the untenability of this conception obvious and to replace it by the idea of continuity. (i) The advance of physiology and the psychology associated with it have shown the connection of mental with that of the nervous system. Too often recognition of connection has stopped short at this point; the older dualism of soul and body has been replaced by that of the brain and the rest of the body. But in fact the nervous system is only a specialized mechanism for keeping all bodily activities working together. Instead of being isolated from them, as an organ of knowing from organs of motor response, it is the organ by which they interact responsively with one another. The brain is essentially an organ for effecting the reciprocal adjustment to each other of the stimuli received from the environment and responses directed upon it." Paragraph 8

"(ii) The development of biology clinches this lesson, with its discovery of evolution. For the philosophic significance of the doctrine of evolution lies precisely in its emphasis upon continuity of simpler and more complex organic forms until we reach man. The development of organic forms begins with structures where the adjustment of environment and organism is obvious, and where anything which can be called mind is at a minimum. As activity becomes more complex, coordinating a greater number of factors in space and time, intelligence plays a more and more marked role, for it has a larger span of the future to forecast and plan for." Paragraph 9

"(iii) The development of the experimental method as the method of getting knowledge and of making sure it is knowledge, and not mere opinion—the method of both discovery and proof—is the remaining great force in bringing about a transformation in the theory of knowledge." Paragraph 10

Dewey wants to establish a continuity between nerve perceptions and the work of the brain, then acknowledge the evolutionary demands on the brain to think with the mind, and see that thinking as development of the mind can be extended and is applicable to a variety of other situations. Nerve perceptions to brain, brain to mind, mind to a variety of application to situations: that's quite a trail!

"The experimental method is new as a scientific resource—as a systematized means of making knowledge, though as old as life as a practical device. Hence it is not surprising that men have not recognized its full scope. For the most part, its significance is regarded as belonging to certain technical and merely physical matters. It will doubtless take a long time to secure the perception that it holds equally as to the forming and testing of ideas in social and moral matters. Men still want the crutch of dogma, of beliefs fixed by authority, to relieve them of the trouble of thinking and the responsibility of directing their activity by thought. They tend to confine their own thinking to a consideration of which one among the rival systems of dogma they will accept. Hence the schools are better adapted, as John Stuart Mill said, to make disciples than inquirers." Paragraph 11

"Schools of Method. There are various systems of philosophy with characteristically different conceptions of the method of knowing. Some of them are named scholasticism, sensationalism, rationalism, idealism, realism, empiricism, transcendentalism, pragmatism, etc…. In brief, the function of knowledge is to make an experience freely available in other experiences. The word 'freely' marks the difference between the principle of knowledge and that of habit. Habit means that an individual undergoes a modification through an experience, which modification forms a predisposition to easier and more effective action in a like direction in the future. Thus it also has the function of making one experience available in subsequent experiences." Today we would probably say we practice with a fluency or skill rather than call our professional development a habit. Paragraph 12

"In other words, knowledge is a perception of those connections of an object which determine its applicability in a given situation…. An ideally perfect knowledge would represent such a network of interconnections that any past experience would offer a point of advantage from which to get at the problem presented in a new experience. In fine, while a habit apart from knowledge supplies us with a single fixed method of attack, knowledge means that selection may be made from a much wider range of habits." Paragraph 13

"While the content of knowledge is what has happened, what it taken as finished and hence settled and sure, the reference of knowledge is future and prospective. For knowledge furnishes the means of understanding or giving meaning to what is still going on and what is to be done…. We cannot entertain the conception of a world in which knowledge of its past would not be helpful in forecasting and giving meaning to its future." Paragraph 15

"The theory of the method of knowing which is advanced in these pages may be termed pragmatic. Its essential feature is to maintain the continuity of knowing with an activity which purposely modifies the environment. It holds that knowledge in its strict sense of something possessed consists of our intellectual resources—of all the habits that render our action intelligent. Only that which has been organized into our disposition so as to enable us to adapt the environment to our needs and to adapt our aims and desires to the situation in which we live is really knowledge. Knowledge is not just something which we are now conscious of, but consists of the dispositions we consciously use in understanding what now happens. Knowledge as an act is bringing some of our dispositions to consciousness with a view to straightening out a perplexity, by conceiving the connection between ourselves and the world in which we live." Paragraph 20

We think. We act. We relate. We reflect, and perhaps reorganize our thought, again and again.

Questions for application

1. Dewey believes that knowledge and his meaning of habit can make facts in relationships applicable to many situations. What has been your experience in developing a repertoire of skills and selecting the most appropriate choice at certain times? (Spontaneous need based choices in teaching practices, for example)

2. Discuss how you feel about John Stuart Mill's statement that schools are more likely to make disciples than inquirers?

3. Do you think people use a scientific approach to determine whether there is sufficient proof before they accept a concept? How can you help students develop the "habit" of scientific scrutiny or inquiry in subjects that are not the hard sciences?

4. Dewey says the essence of studying history is to be oriented to the future and to be prospective. How many history classes have you attended that made you project your thinking into the future? How would you teach students to think prospectively?

Notes and Quotes:

Chapter 26:
Theories of Morals

Dewey wants individuals to "engage in a progressively cumulative undertaking under conditions which engage their interest and require their reflection. For only in such cases is it possible that the disposition of desire and thinking should be an organic factor in overt and obvious conduct. Given a consecutive activity embodying the student's own interest, where a definite result is to be obtained, and where neither routine habit nor the following of dictated directions nor capricious improvising will suffice, and there rise of conscious purpose, conscious desire, and deliberate reflection are inevitable. They are inevitable as the spirit and quality of an activity having specific consequences, not as forming an isolated realm of inner consciousness." If you know what needs to be done, and you want to do it, and you think as you go, you will accomplish the learning goal. But it has to be a new technique, exploring your way through it and not doing it carelessly. Paragraph 10

"2. The Opposition of Duty and Interest. Probably there is not antithesis more often set up in moral discussion than that between acting from 'principle' and from 'interest'. To act on principle is to act disinterestedly, according to general law, which is above all personal considerations. To act according to interest is, so the allegation runs, to act selfishly, with one's own personal profit in view." Paragraph 11

"Both sides assume that the self is a fixed and hence isolated quantity. As a consequence, there is a rigid dilemma between acting for an interest of the self and without interest. If the self is something fixed antecedent to action, then acting from interest means trying to get more in the way of possessions for the self--whether in the way of fame, approval of others, power over others, pecuniary profit, or pleasure.... Then the reaction from this view as a cynical depreciation of human nature leads to the view that men who act nobly act with no interest at all. Yet to an unbiased judgment it would appear plain that a man must be interested in what he is doing or he would not do it.... The moment we recognize that the self is not something ready-made, but something in continuous formation through choice of action, the whole situation clears up. A man's interest in keeping at his work in spite of danger to life means that his self is found in that work; if he finally gave up, and preferred his personal safety or comfort, it would mean that he preferred to be that kind of a self. The mistake lies in making a separation between interest and self, and supposing that the latter is the end to which interest in objects and acts and others is a mere means. In fact, self and interest are two names for the same fact; the kind and amount of interest actively taken in a thing reveals and measures the quality of selfhood which exists. Bear in mind that interest means the active or moving identity of the self with a certain object, and the whole alleged dilemma falls to the ground." Paragraph 13

"(i) The generous self consciously identifies itself with the full range of relationships implied in its activity, instead of drawing a sharp line between itself and considerations which are excluded as alien or indifferent; (ii) it readjusts and expands its past ideas of itself to take in new consequences as they become perceptible... The wider or larger self which means inclusion instead of denial of relationships is identical with a self which enlarges in order to assume previously unforeseen ties." Growing awareness creates growing commitments or connections. Paragraph 14

"Assuming, however, that school conditions are such as to provide desirable occupations, it is interest in the occupation as a whole—that is, in its continuous development—which keeps a pupil at his work in spite of temporary diversions and unpleasant obstacles." Paragraph 15

"Moral education in school is practically hopeless when we set up the development of character as a supreme end, and at the same time treat the acquiring of knowledge and the development of understanding, which of necessity occupy the chief part of school time, as having nothing to do with character. On such a basis, moral education is inevitably reduced to some kind of catechetical instruction, or lessons about morals. Lessons 'about morals' signify as matter of course lessons in what other people think about virtues and duties. It amounts to something only in the degree in which pupils happen to be already animated by sympathetic and dignified regard for the sentiments of others. Without such a regard, it has no more influence on character than in formation about the mountains of Asia; with a service regard, it increases dependence upon others, and throws upon those in authority the responsibility for conduct. As a matter of fact, direct instruction in morals has been effective only in social groups where it was a part of the authoritative control of the many by the few. Not the teaching as such but the reinforcement of it by the whole regime of which it was an incident made it effective." Paragraph 17

"What is learned and employed in an occupation having an aim and involving cooperation with others is moral knowledge, whether consciously so regarded or not. For it builds up a social interest and confers the intelligence needed to make that interest effective in practice. Just because the studies of the curriculum represent standard factors in social life, they are organs of initiation into social values. As mere school studies, their acquisition has only a technical worth. Acquired under conditions where their social significance is realized, they feed moral interest and develop moral insight. Moreover, the qualities of mind discussed under the topic of method of learning are all of them intrinsically moral qualities. Open-mindedness, single-mindedness, sincerity, breadth of outlook, thoroughness, assumption of responsibility for developing the consequences of ideas which are accepted, are moral traits." Paragraph 20

"All of the separations which we have been criticizing—and which the idea of education set forth in the previous chapters is designed to avoid—spring from taking morals too narrowly,--giving them, on one side, a sentimental goody-goody turn without reference to effective ability to do what is socially needed, and, on the other side, overemphasizing convention and tradition so as to limit morals to a list of definitely stated acts. As a matter of fact, morals are as broad as acts which concern our relationships with others. And potentially this includes all our acts, even though their social bearing may not be thought of at the time of performance. For every act, by the principle of habit, modifies disposition—it sets up a certain kind of inclination and desire." Dewey would no doubt agree that moral behavior based on reasons, rather than rules, is more dependable behavior. It is harder to break a reason, than it is to break a rule. Paragraph 21

"The moral and the social quality of conduct are, in the last analysis, identical with each other…. And the great danger which threatens school work is the absence of conditions which make possible a permeating social spirit; this is the great enemy of effective moral training. For this spirit can be actively present only when certain conditions are met." Paragraph 22

"(i) In the first place, the school must itself be a community life in all which that implies. Social perceptions and interests can be developed only in a genuinely social medium—one where there is give and take in the building up of a common experience…. Playgrounds, shops, workrooms, laboratories not only direct the natural active tendencies of youth, but they involve intercourse, communication, and cooperation,--all extending the perception of connections." Paragraph 23

"(ii) The learning in school should be continuous with that out of school. There should be a free interplay between the two. This is possible only when there are numerous points of contact between the social interests of the one and of the other." Paragraph 24

"A narrow and moralistic view of morals is responsible for the failure to recognize that all the aims and values which are desirable in education are themselves moral. Discipline, natural development, culture, social efficiency, are moral traits—marks of a person who is a worthy member of that society which it is the business of education to further." Paragraph 25

"All education which develops power to share effectively in social life is moral. It forms character which not only does the particular deed socially necessary but one which is interested in that continuous readjustment which is essential to growth. Interest in learning from all the contacts of life is the essential moral interest." Paragraph 27

Questions for application

1. People live according to their own moral compass. For Dewey developing character means developing life-style. How does character education in the schools today reflect the consistent commitment to personal transformation expressed through consistent actions?

2. Concern for the environment is a very obvious expression of personal interests that have a social application. But at a more individual level or classroom level, how does social interaction influence applied moral development?

3. What does the term social efficiency mean to you?

4. In the first paragraph Dewey describes what is needed to create purpose, desire and reflection. What is needed for that, and what potential detractors must we be aware of? How would you certify a student's project as centered in the right direction?

Notes and Quotes:

Epilogue

At this point, what John Dewey believes about Democracy and Education is not an issue. What is an issue should be what your response to John Dewey is. His expectation would be that you were moved in some ways by his comments. He would expect being moved would result in change in your philosophical approach to education and in your educational practice.

He would look for a body of evidence that you are undergoing reflection and expansion in what you do. He would look for transparency in your evidence to see behind it, to see what effect you have on society and how you have allowed society to inform you. And he would search in the background for diversity.

He asks you to be open, curious, industrious, purposeful, reflective, sensitive, pragmatic, contributing and coaching.

Students have sometimes wondered why education still falls short of Dewey's views. Perhaps the answer is the same as what he saw as distractions at his time. Academic aloofness, task training without understanding, traditional approaches, social classes, scarcity of resources, lack of access in governance and business interests were all concerns in 1916, and they have been since then, as well.

A better question is: why isn't Dewey more evident in your classroom or your school? There are schools where staff don't chew gum if students can't. There are schools where para-professionals participate in staff discussions freely. There are classes where students develop individual extensive cross-curricular projects. There are classrooms where students conduct behavior management. Democracy happens in many ways. Does it happen near you?

The Conclusion is also Your Challenge:

When we combine the continuous development of the learner with the continuous mutual stimulation of a democratic social system, you have a Hegelian optimism that education is the free and dynamic force behind democratic social improvement, enriched by diversity.

Citations regarding John Dewey include but are not limited to the following:

Olson, S. (2005, August 25) *John Dewey—American Pragmatic Philosopher* retrieved from website http://johndewey.shawnolson.net

Smith, Mark K (2001) *john dewey* retrieved from website http://www.infed.org/thinkers/et-dewey.htm

The Columbia Encyclopedia, Sixth Edition, 2003, Columbia University Press: People: John Dewey

Discussion Paper Submission retrieved from website http://philosophy.uncc.edu/mleldrid/SAAP/MSU/DP04.html

John Dewey in Wikipedia retrieved Jan 7, 2009 from http://www.bing.com/reference/sem.html/John_Dewey#s8

Made in the USA
Las Vegas, NV
05 January 2023

65078351R00072